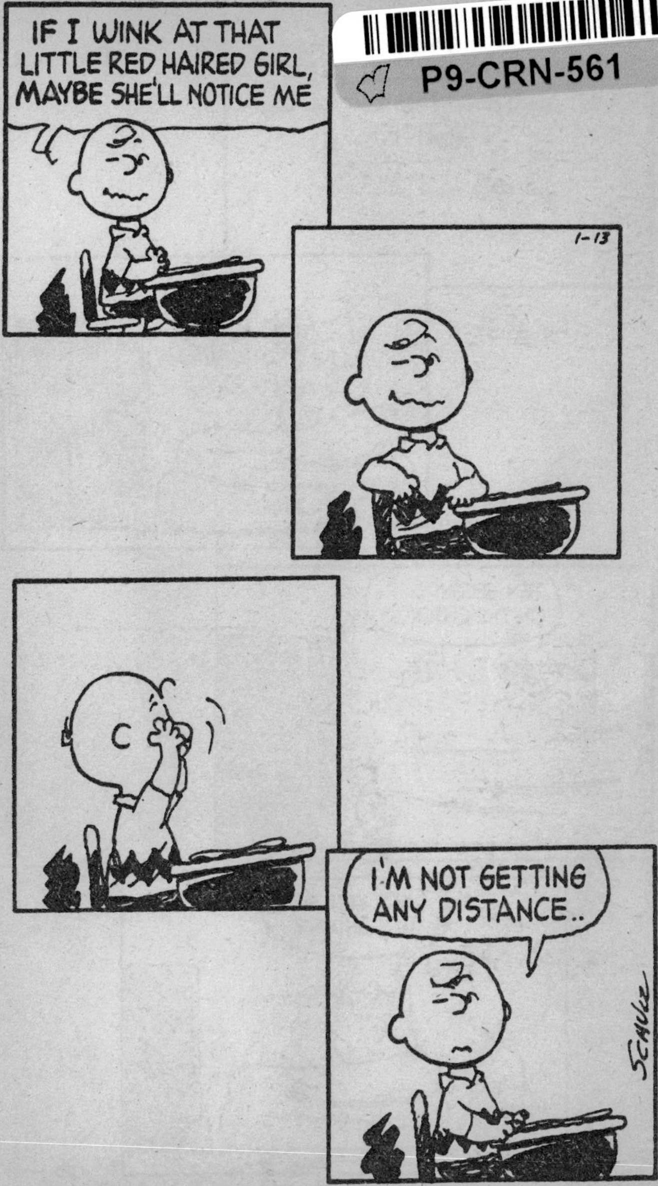
IF I WINK AT THAT LITTLE RED HAIRED GIRL, MAYBE SHE'LL NOTICE ME
1-13
I'M NOT GETTING ANY DISTANCE..
SCHULZ

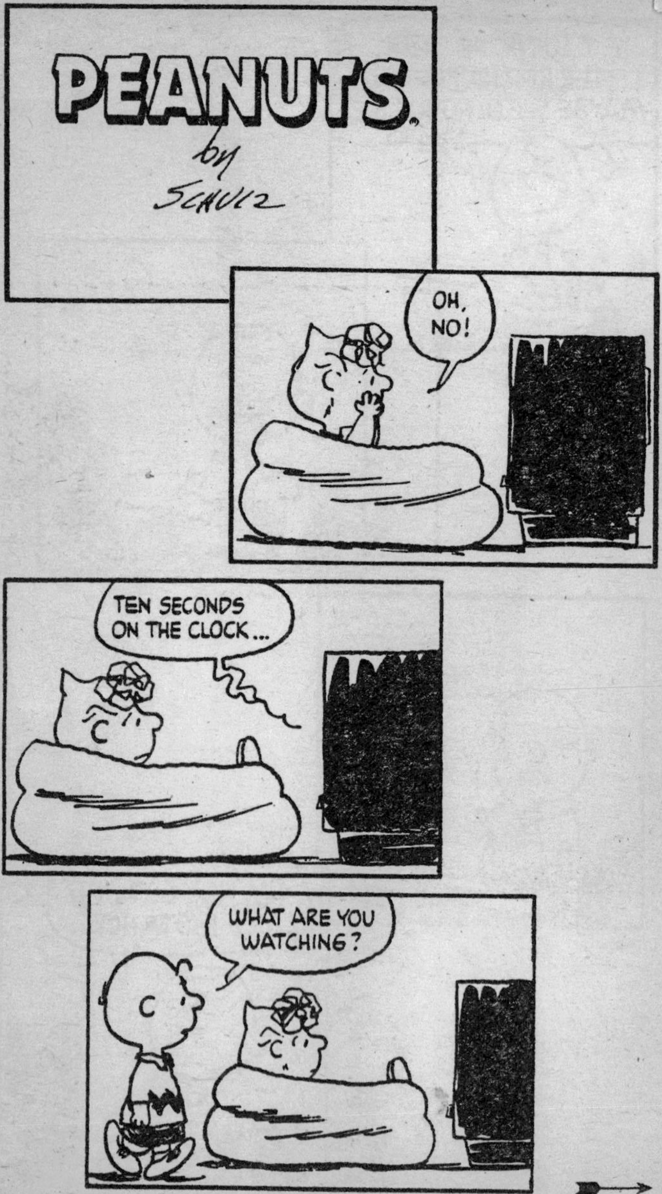
PEANUTS
by SCHULZ
OH, NO!
TEN SECONDS ON THE CLOCK...
WHAT ARE YOU WATCHING?

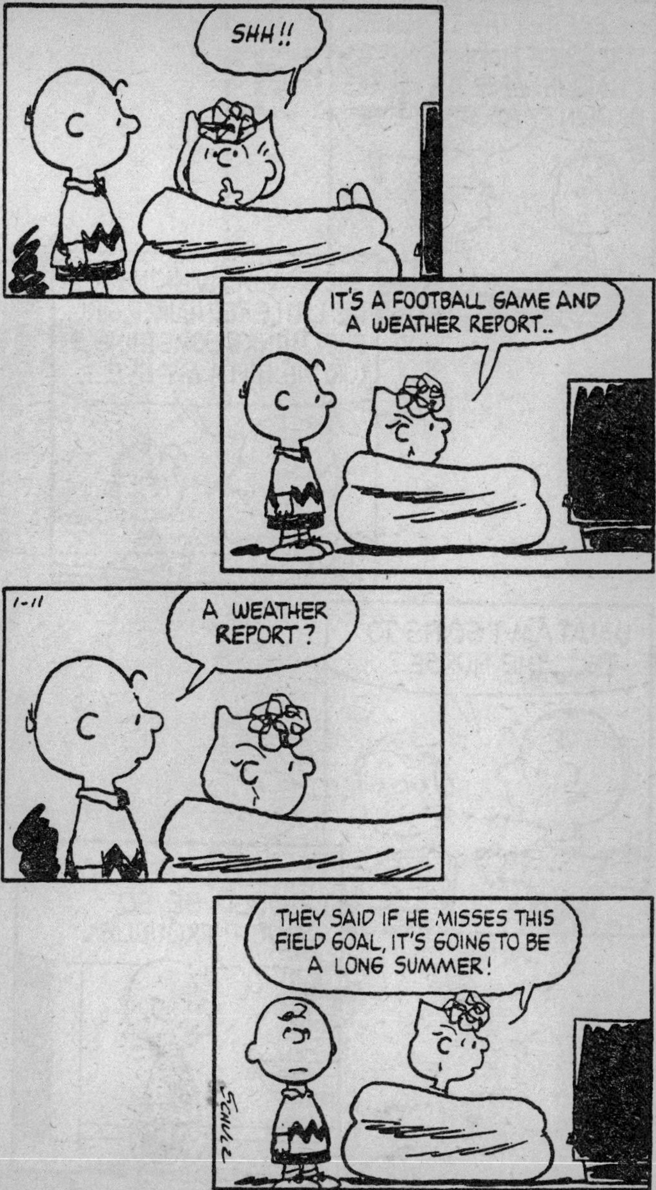
SHH!!
IT'S A FOOTBALL GAME AND A WEATHER REPORT..
1-11
A WEATHER REPORT?
THEY SAID IF HE MISSES THIS FIELD GOAL, IT'S GOING TO BE A LONG SUMMER!
SCHULZ

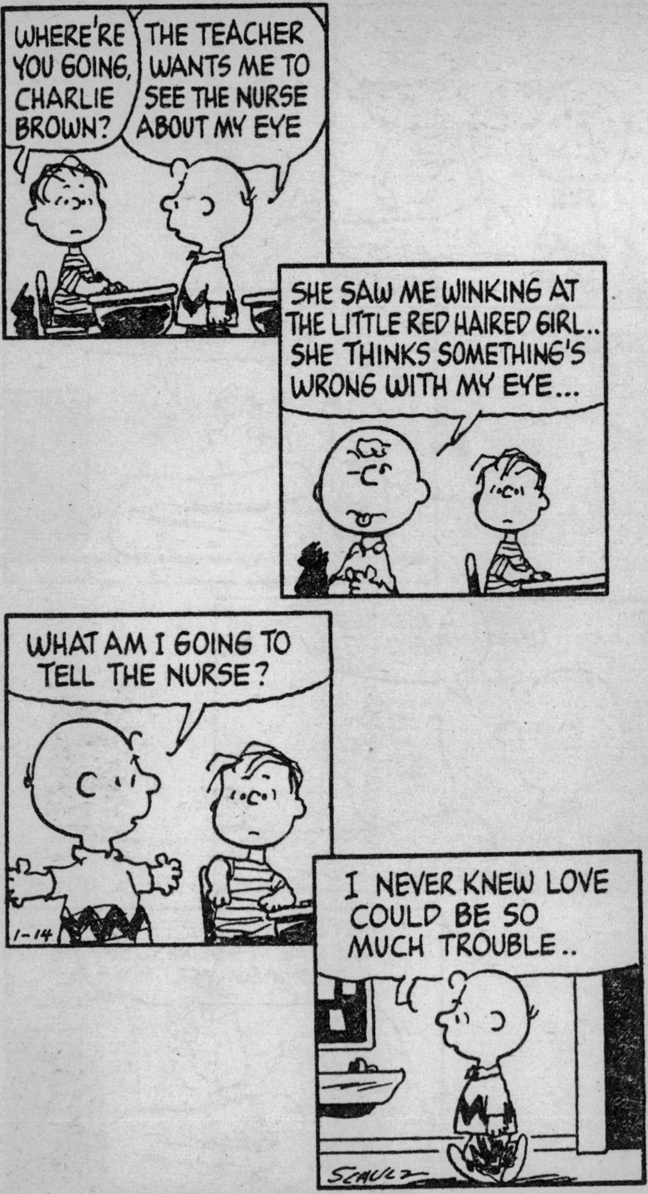
WHERE'RE YOU GOING, CHARLIE BROWN?
THE TEACHER WANTS ME TO SEE THE NURSE ABOUT MY EYE
SHE SAW ME WINKING AT THE LITTLE RED HAIRED GIRL.. SHE THINKS SOMETHING'S WRONG WITH MY EYE...
WHAT AM I GOING TO TELL THE NURSE?
1-14
I NEVER KNEW LOVE COULD BE SO MUCH TROUBLE..
SCHULZ

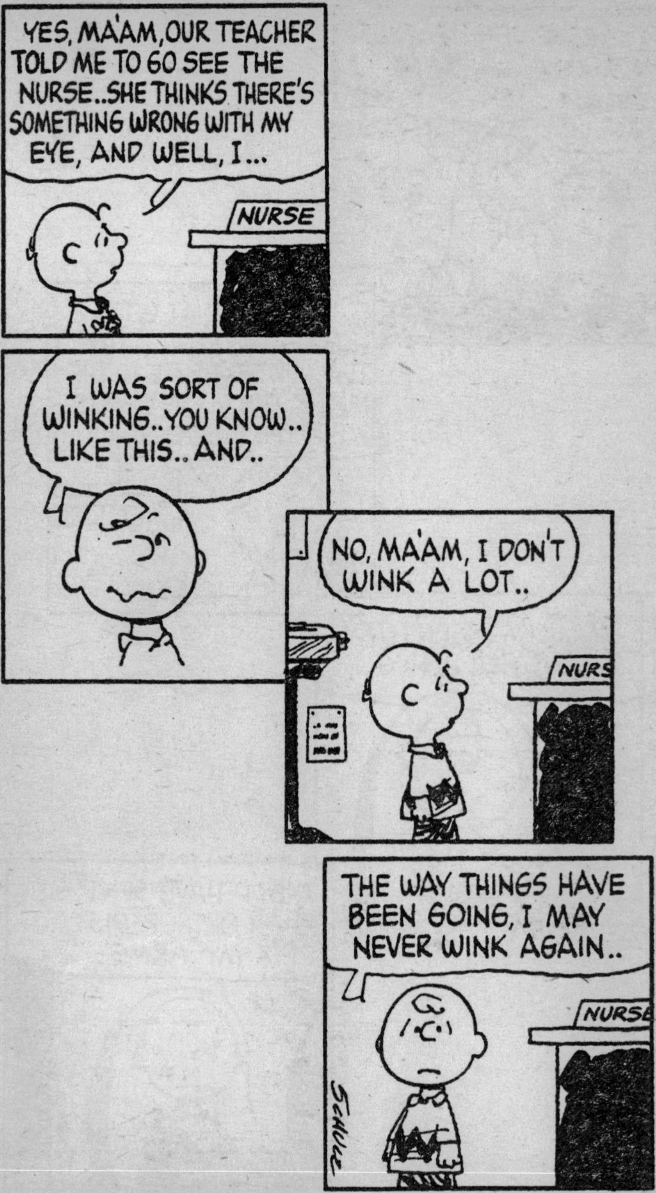
YES, MA'AM, OUR TEACHER TOLD ME TO GO SEE THE NURSE..SHE THINKS THERE'S SOMETHING WRONG WITH MY EYE, AND WELL, I...
NURSE
I WAS SORT OF WINKING..YOU KNOW.. LIKE THIS.. AND..
NO, MA'AM, I DON'T WINK A LOT..
THE WAY THINGS HAVE BEEN GOING, I MAY NEVER WINK AGAIN..
SCHULZ

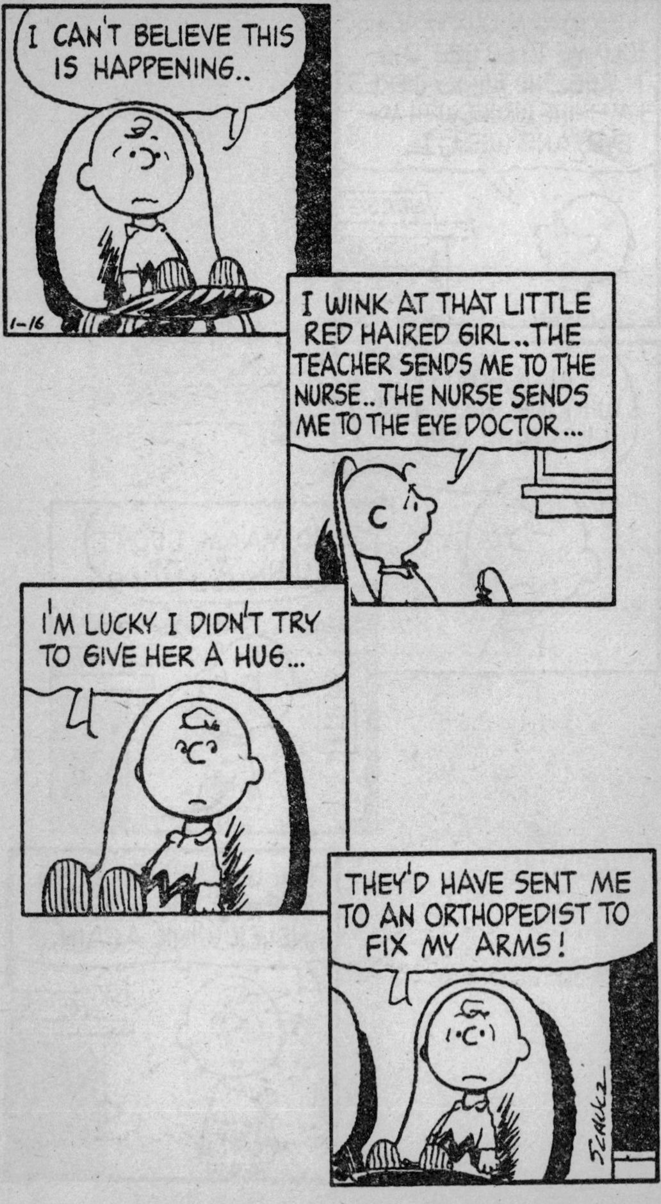
I CAN'T BELIEVE THIS IS HAPPENING..
1-16
I WINK AT THAT LITTLE RED HAIRED GIRL..THE TEACHER SENDS ME TO THE NURSE..THE NURSE SENDS ME TO THE EYE DOCTOR...
I'M LUCKY I DIDN'T TRY TO GIVE HER A HUG...
THEY'D HAVE SENT ME TO AN ORTHOPEDIST TO FIX MY ARMS!
SCHULZ

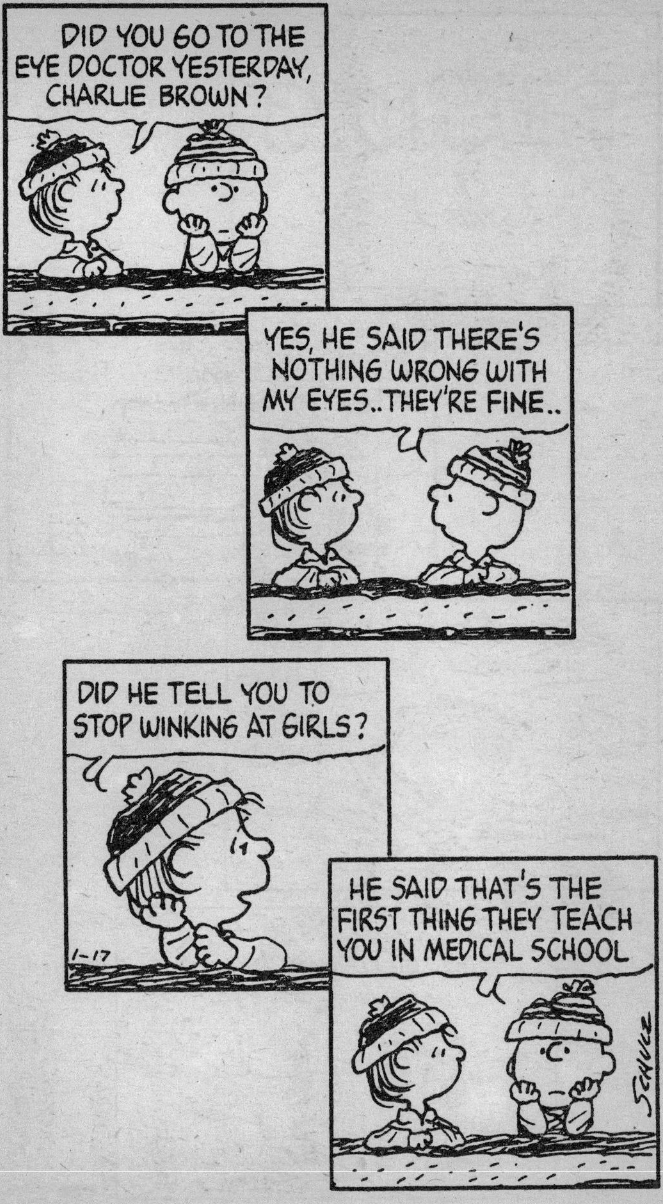
DID YOU GO TO THE EYE DOCTOR YESTERDAY, CHARLIE BROWN?
YES, HE SAID THERE'S NOTHING WRONG WITH MY EYES..THEY'RE FINE..
DID HE TELL YOU TO STOP WINKING AT GIRLS?
1-17
HE SAID THAT'S THE FIRST THING THEY TEACH YOU IN MEDICAL SCHOOL
SCHULZ

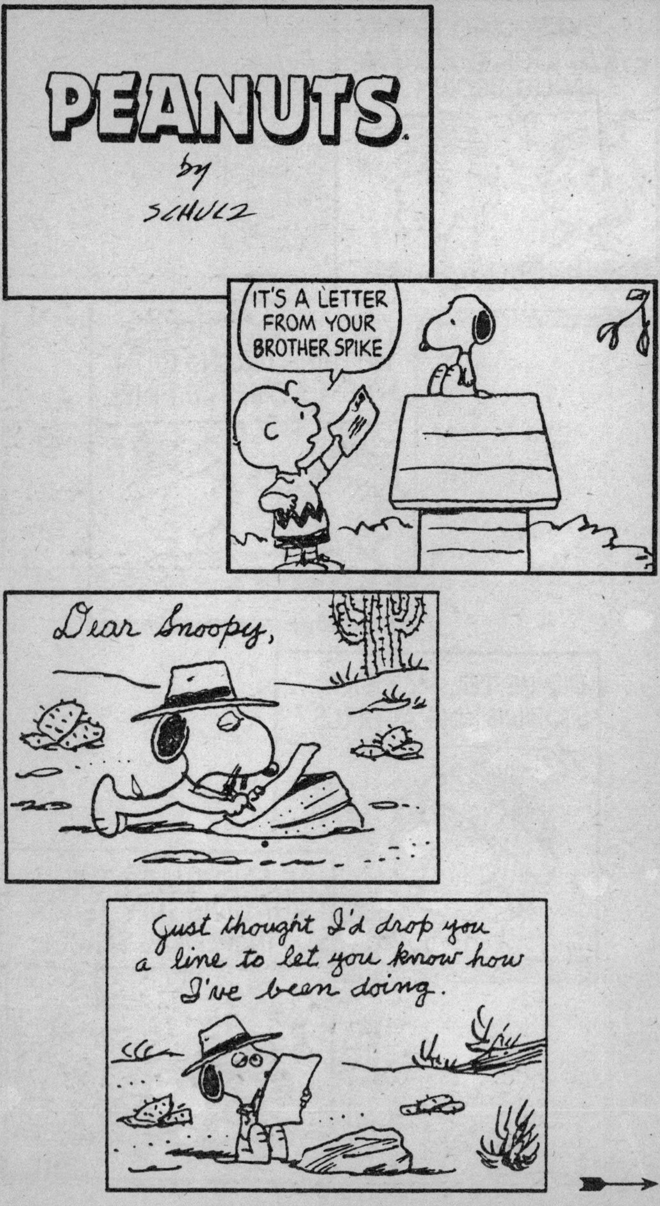
PEANUTS
by SCHULZ
IT'S A LETTER FROM YOUR BROTHER SPIKE
Dear Snoopy,
Just thought I'd drop you a line to let you know how I've been doing.

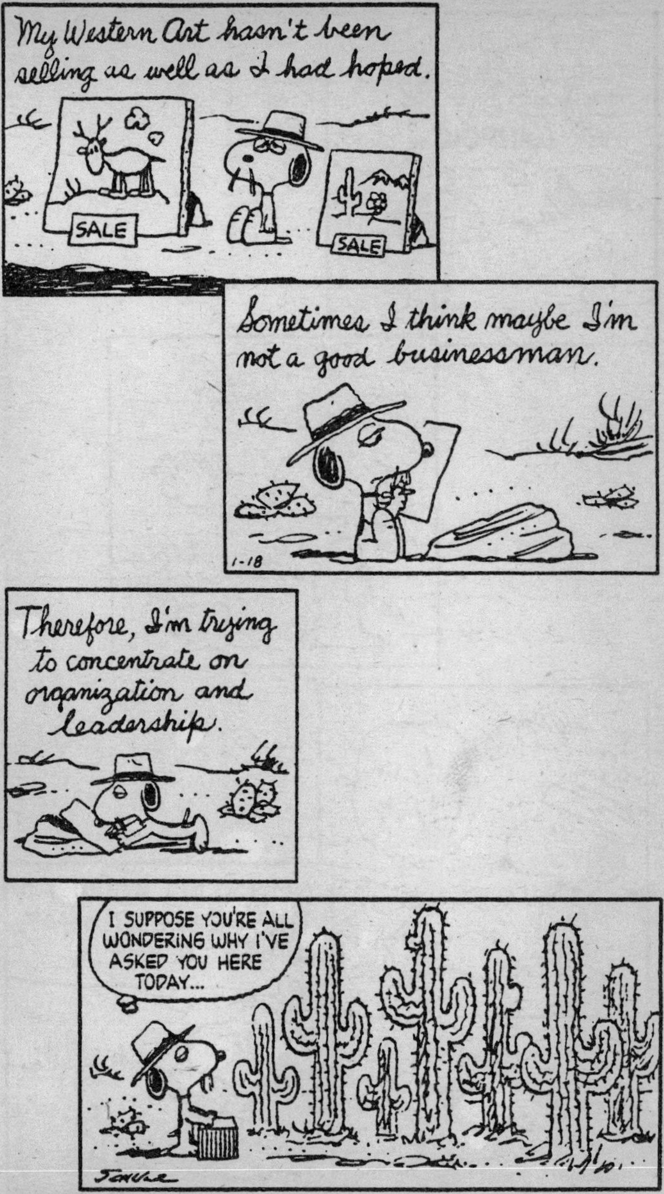
My Western Art hasn't been selling as well as I had hoped.
SALE
SALE
Sometimes I think maybe I'm not a good businessman.
1-18
Therefore, I'm trying to concentrate on organization and leadership.
I SUPPOSE YOU'RE ALL WONDERING WHY I'VE ASKED YOU HERE TODAY...

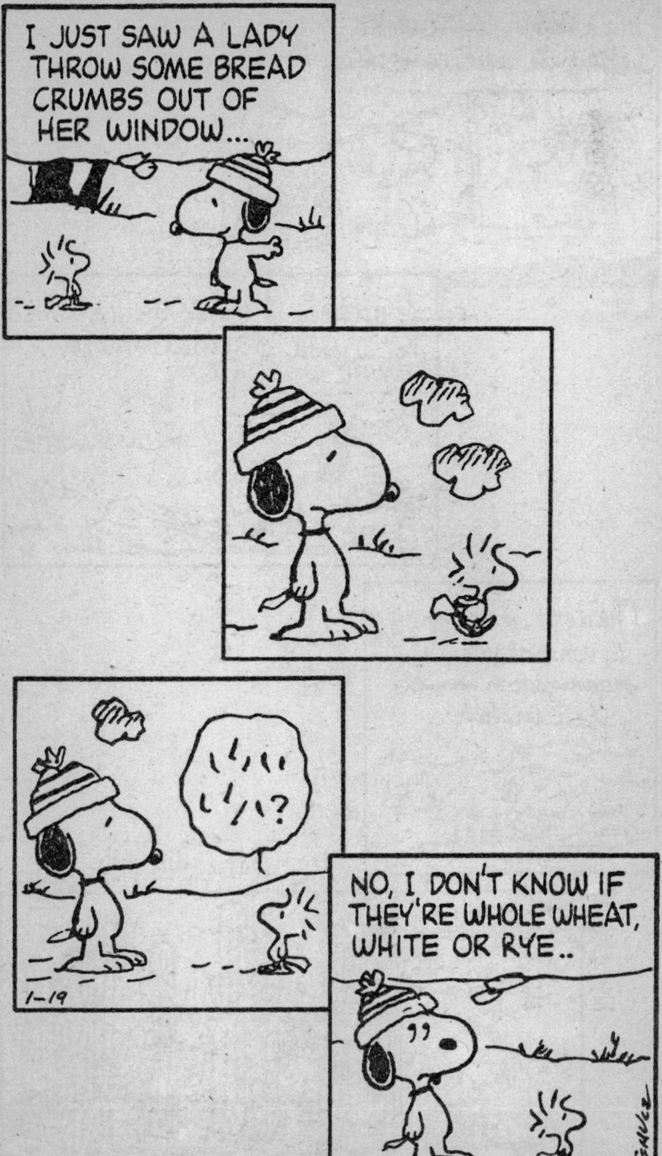
I JUST SAW A LADY THROW SOME BREAD CRUMBS OUT OF HER WINDOW...
?
1-19
NO, I DON'T KNOW IF THEY'RE WHOLE WHEAT, WHITE OR RYE..
SCHULZ

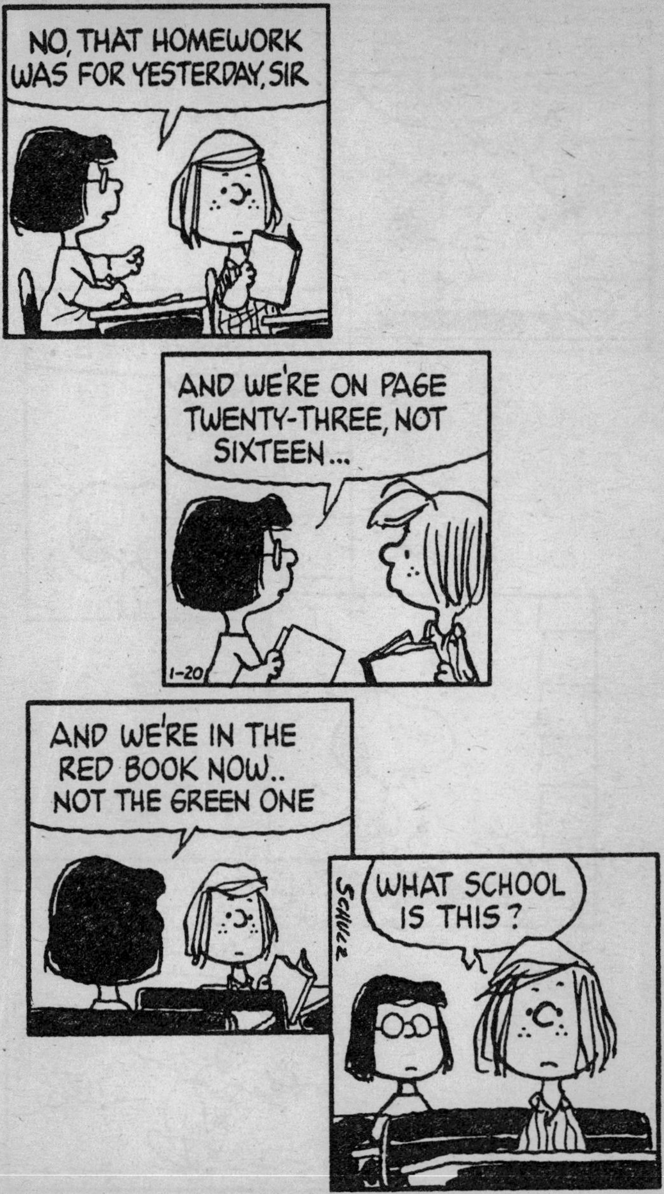
NO, THAT HOMEWORK WAS FOR YESTERDAY, SIR
AND WE'RE ON PAGE TWENTY-THREE, NOT SIXTEEN...
1-20
AND WE'RE IN THE RED BOOK NOW.. NOT THE GREEN ONE
SCHULZ
WHAT SCHOOL IS THIS?

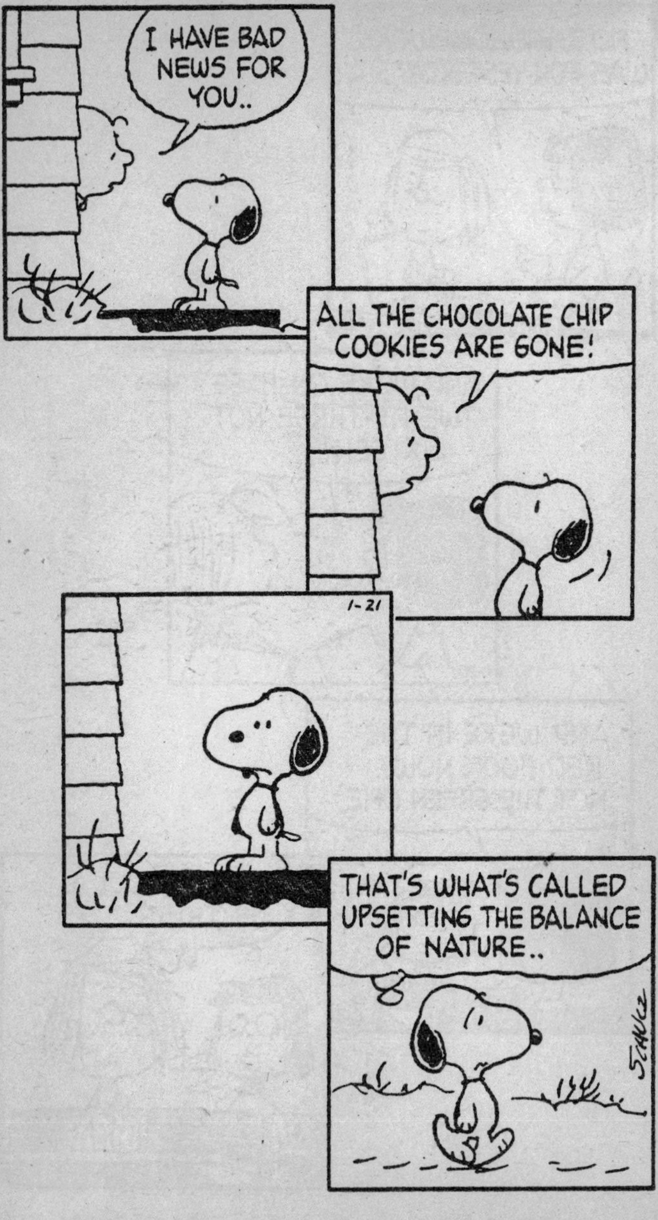
I HAVE BAD NEWS FOR YOU..
ALL THE CHOCOLATE CHIP COOKIES ARE GONE!
1-21
THAT'S WHAT'S CALLED UPSETTING THE BALANCE OF NATURE..
SCHULZ

YOU AND THAT STUPID BLANKET!
WHAT ARE YOU GOING TO DO WHEN YOU GROW UP?
1-22
WHAT WILL YOU DO WITH IT THEN?
IT'LL LOOK GREAT WITH A TUXEDO!
SCHULZ

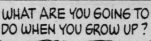

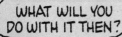

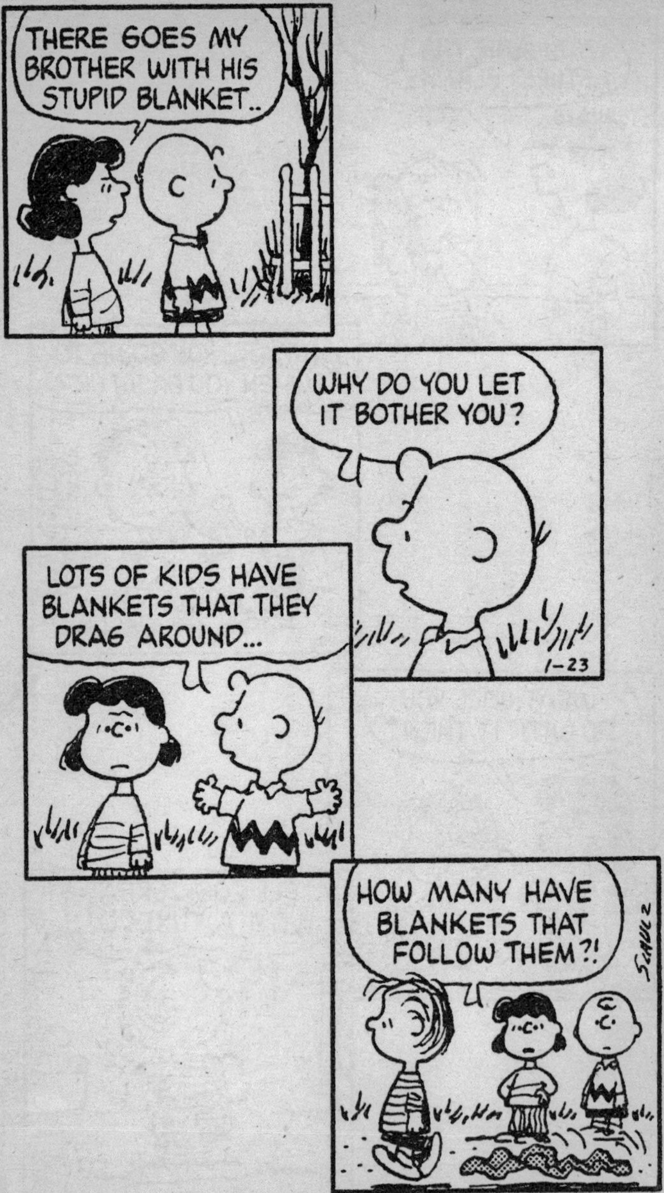
THERE GOES MY BROTHER WITH HIS STUPID BLANKET..
WHY DO YOU LET IT BOTHER YOU?
1-23
LOTS OF KIDS HAVE BLANKETS THAT THEY DRAG AROUND...
HOW MANY HAVE BLANKETS THAT FOLLOW THEM?!
SCHULZ

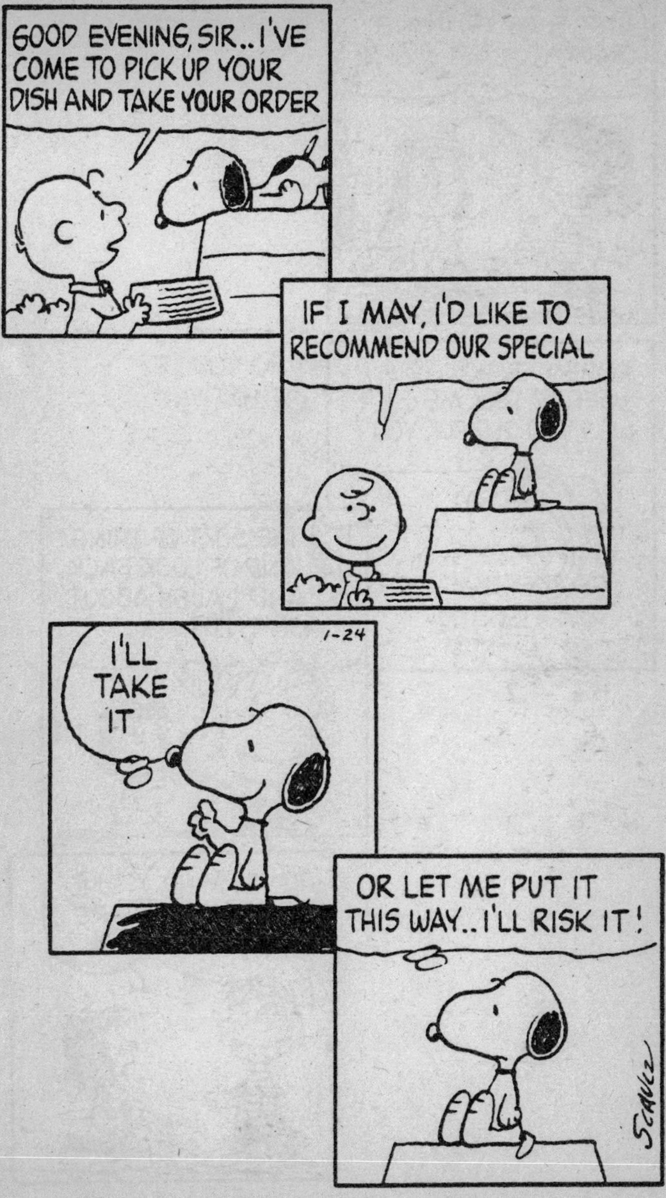
GOOD EVENING, SIR.. I'VE COME TO PICK UP YOUR DISH AND TAKE YOUR ORDER
IF I MAY, I'D LIKE TO RECOMMEND OUR SPECIAL
1-24
I'LL TAKE IT
OR LET ME PUT IT THIS WAY.. I'LL RISK IT!
SCHULZ

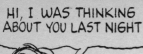

HI, I WAS THINKING ABOUT YOU LAST NIGHT

REMEMBER HOW YOU USED TO TELL ME I WAS TOO OLD FOR YOU?

1-26

IT'S THE SORT OF THING WE KIND OF LOOK BACK ON AND LAUGH ABOUT, ISN'T IT?

DO YOU MIND IF I SIT DOWN?

WHO ARE YOU?

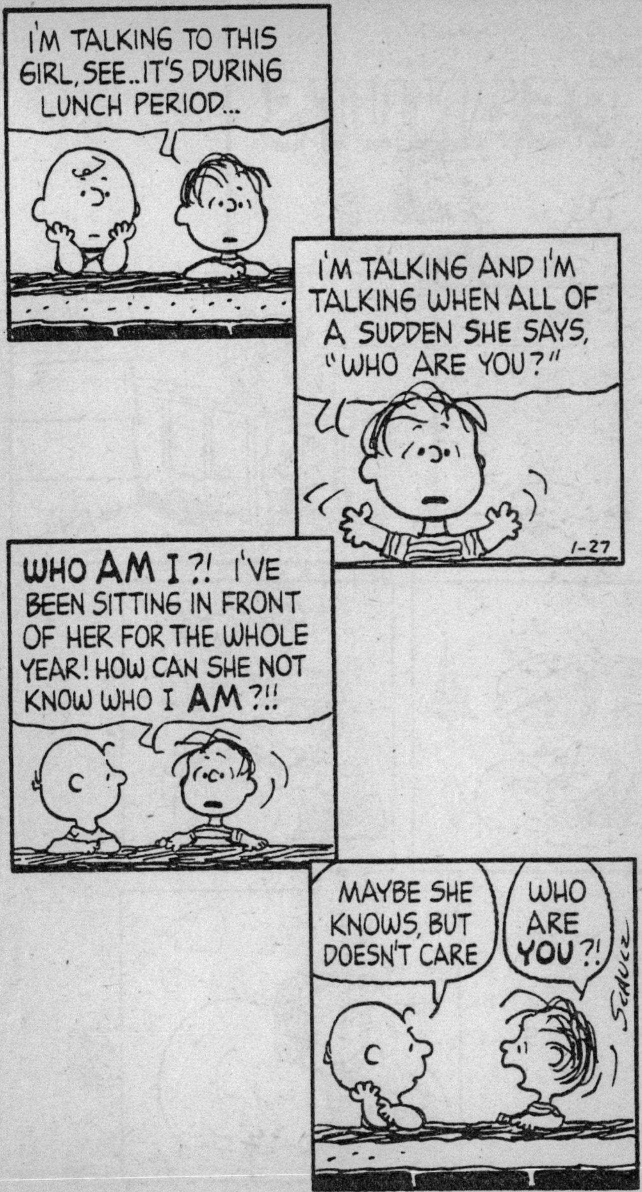
I'M TALKING TO THIS GIRL, SEE...IT'S DURING LUNCH PERIOD...
I'M TALKING AND I'M TALKING WHEN ALL OF A SUDDEN SHE SAYS, "WHO ARE YOU?"
1-27
WHO AM I ?! I'VE BEEN SITTING IN FRONT OF HER FOR THE WHOLE YEAR! HOW CAN SHE NOT KNOW WHO I AM ?!!
MAYBE SHE KNOWS, BUT DOESN'T CARE
WHO ARE YOU ?!
SCHULZ

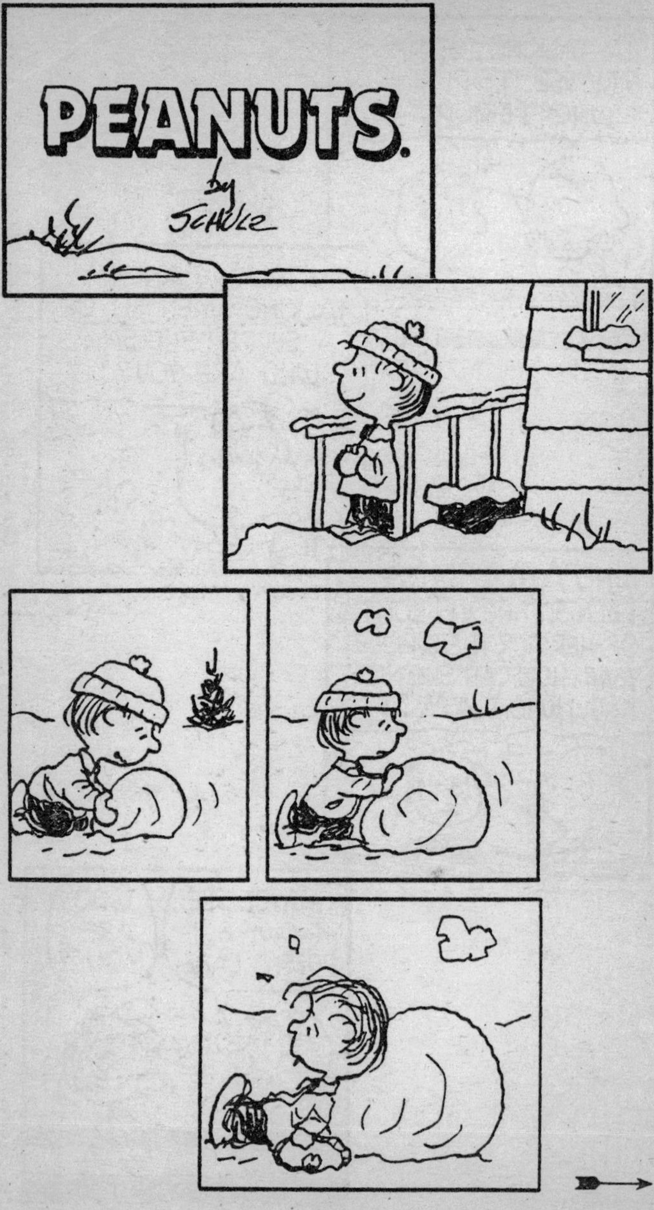
PEANUTS.
by SCHULZ

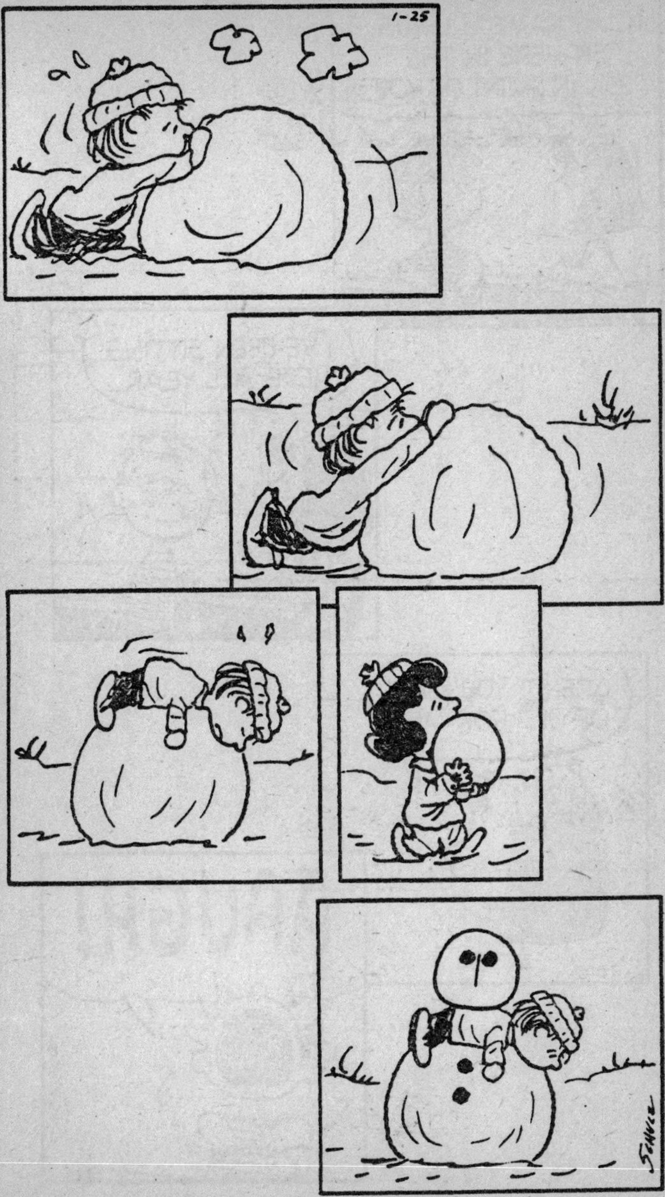
1-25
SCHULZ

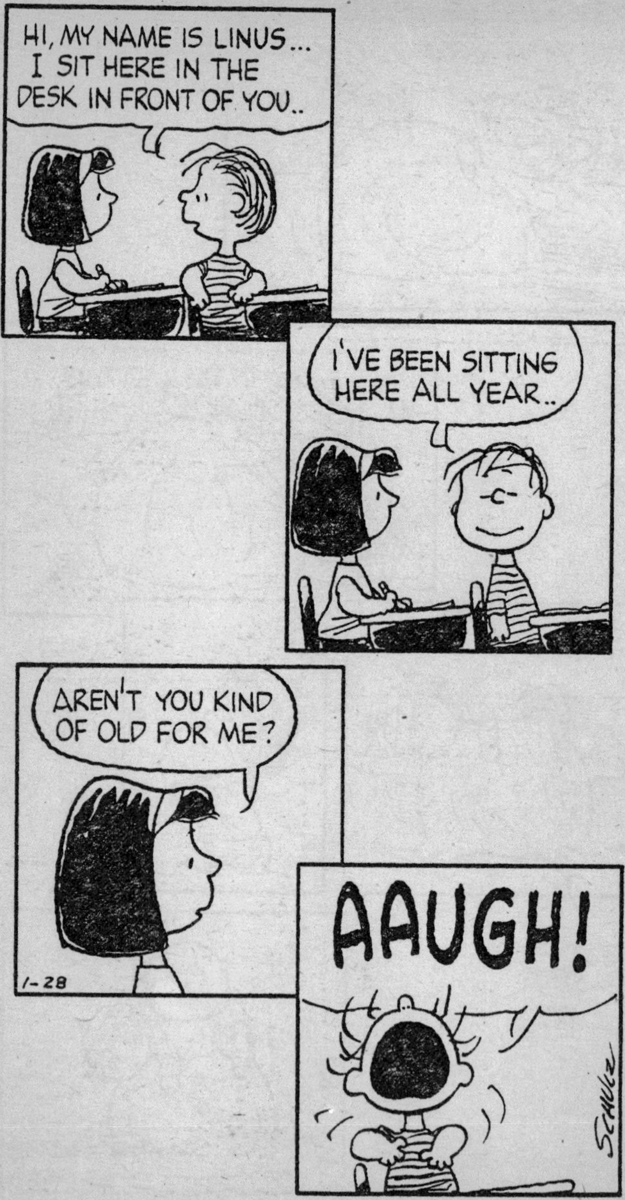
HI, MY NAME IS LINUS... I SIT HERE IN THE DESK IN FRONT OF YOU..
I'VE BEEN SITTING HERE ALL YEAR..
AREN'T YOU KIND OF OLD FOR ME?
1-28
AAUGH!
SCHULZ

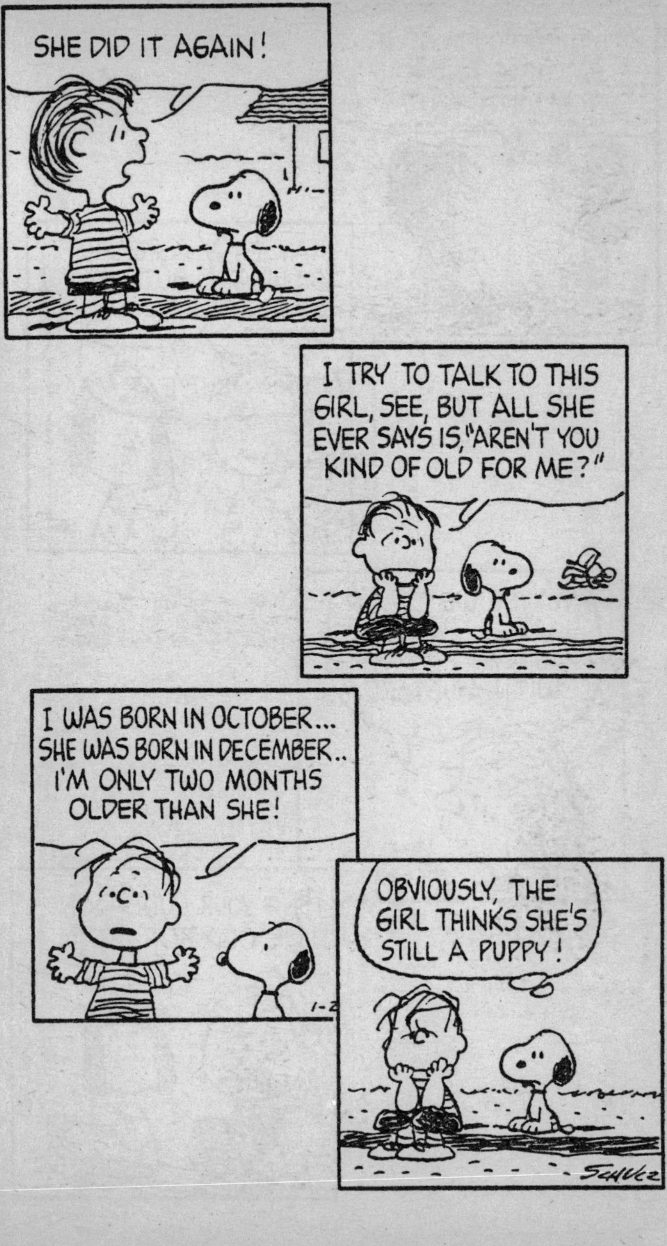
SHE DID IT AGAIN!
I TRY TO TALK TO THIS GIRL, SEE, BUT ALL SHE EVER SAYS IS, "AREN'T YOU KIND OF OLD FOR ME?"
I WAS BORN IN OCTOBER... SHE WAS BORN IN DECEMBER.. I'M ONLY TWO MONTHS OLDER THAN SHE!
OBVIOUSLY, THE GIRL THINKS SHE'S STILL A PUPPY!
SCHULZ

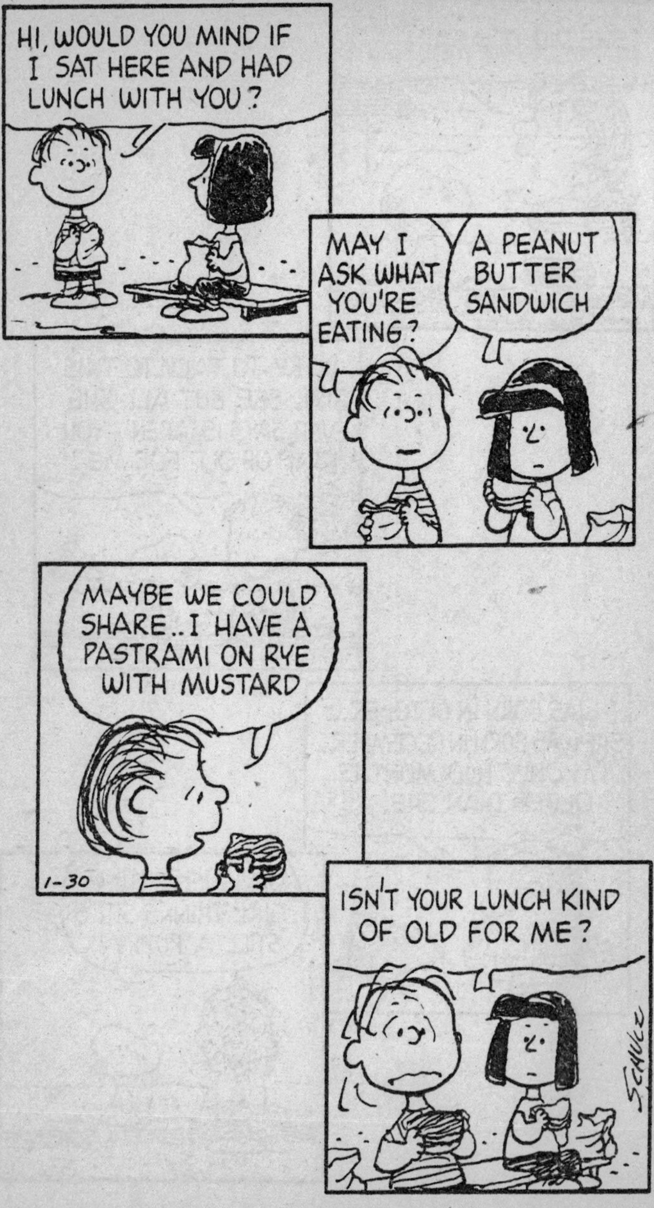
HI, WOULD YOU MIND IF I SAT HERE AND HAD LUNCH WITH YOU?
MAY I ASK WHAT YOU'RE EATING?
A PEANUT BUTTER SANDWICH
MAYBE WE COULD SHARE..I HAVE A PASTRAMI ON RYE WITH MUSTARD
1-30
ISN'T YOUR LUNCH KIND OF OLD FOR ME?
SCHULZ

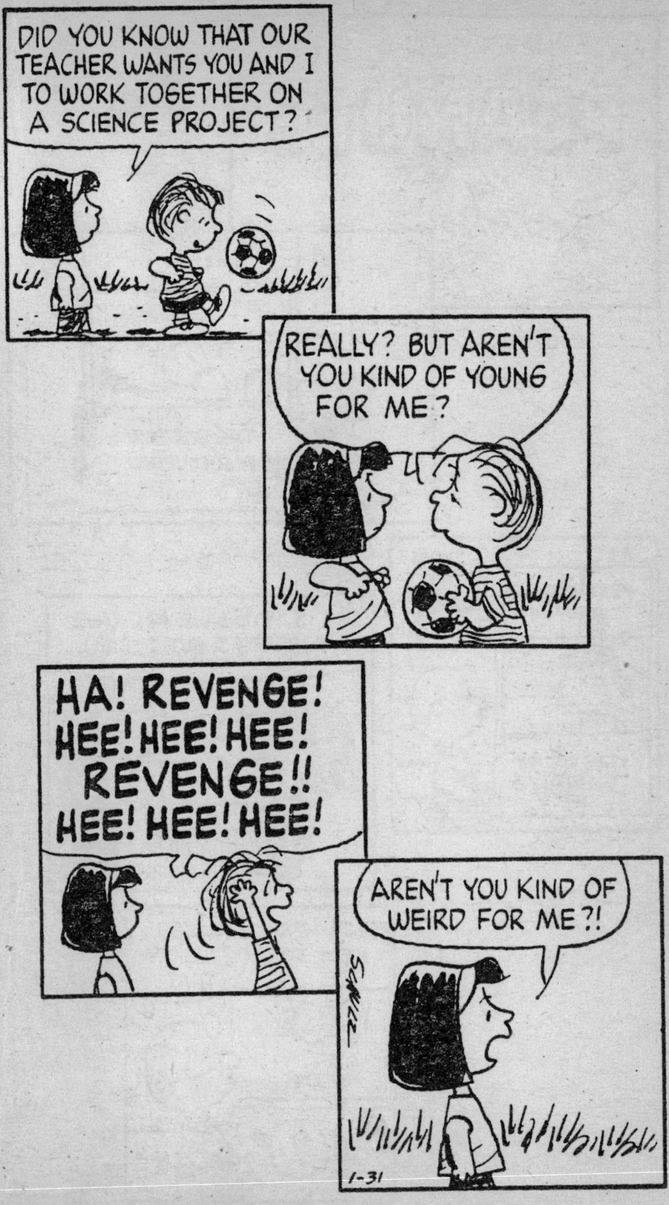
DID YOU KNOW THAT OUR TEACHER WANTS YOU AND I TO WORK TOGETHER ON A SCIENCE PROJECT?
REALLY? BUT AREN'T YOU KIND OF YOUNG FOR ME?
HA! REVENGE! HEE! HEE! HEE! REVENGE!! HEE! HEE! HEE!
AREN'T YOU KIND OF WEIRD FOR ME?!
SCHULZ
1-31

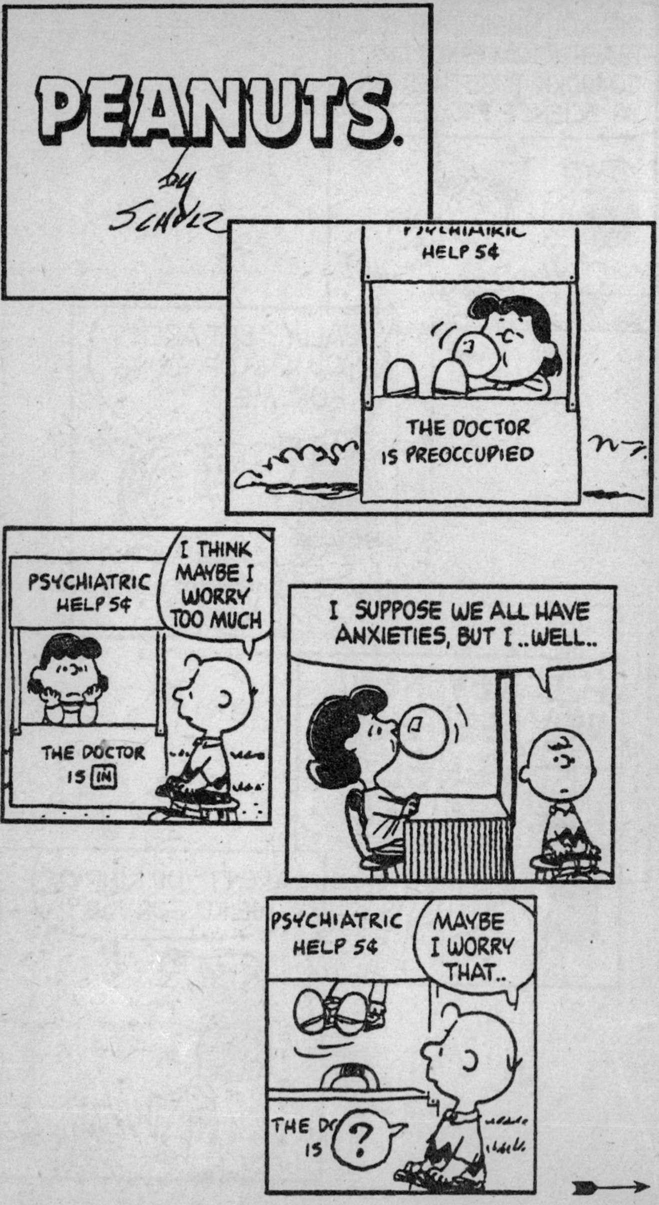
PEANUTS.
by SCHULZ
HELP 5¢
THE DOCTOR IS PREOCCUPIED
PSYCHIATRIC HELP 5¢
I THINK MAYBE I WORRY TOO MUCH
THE DOCTOR IS IN
I SUPPOSE WE ALL HAVE ANXIETIES, BUT I ..WELL..
PSYCHIATRIC HELP 5¢
MAYBE I WORRY THAT..
THE DO
IS
?

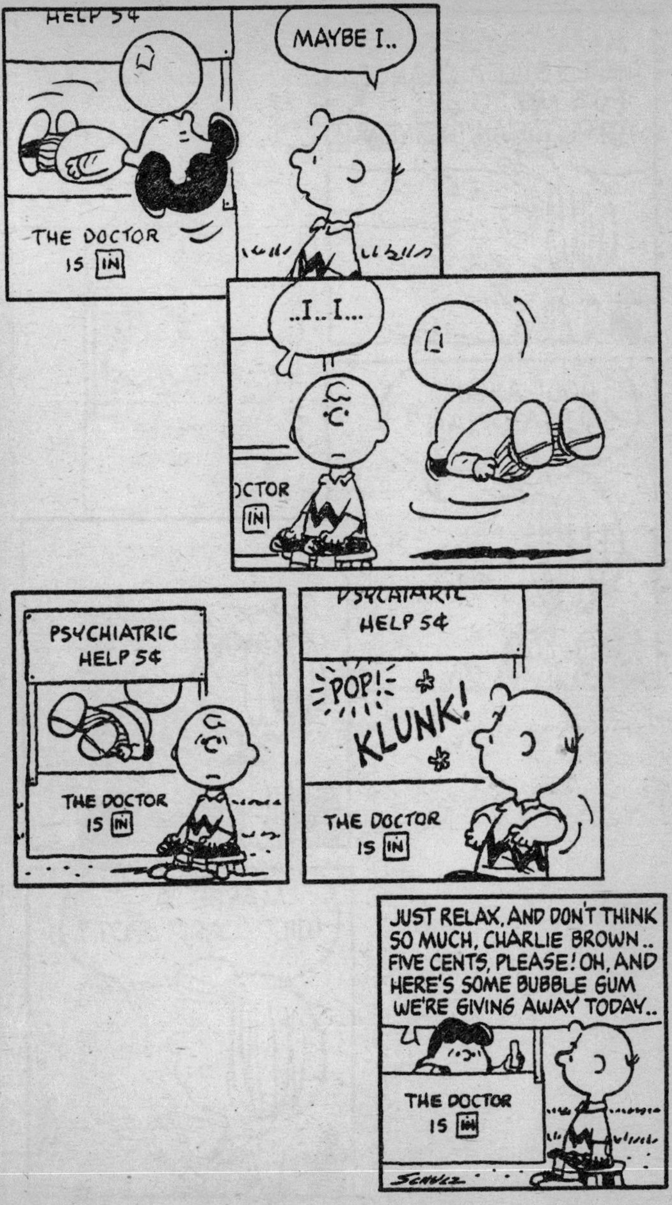

HELP 5¢
THE DOCTOR IS IN
MAYBE I..
..I.. I...
PSYCHIATRIC HELP 5¢
THE DOCTOR IS IN
HELP 5¢
POP!
KLUNK!
THE DOCTOR IS IN
JUST RELAX, AND DON'T THINK SO MUCH, CHARLIE BROWN.. FIVE CENTS, PLEASE! OH, AND HERE'S SOME BUBBLE GUM WE'RE GIVING AWAY TODAY..
THE DOCTOR IS IN
SCHULZ

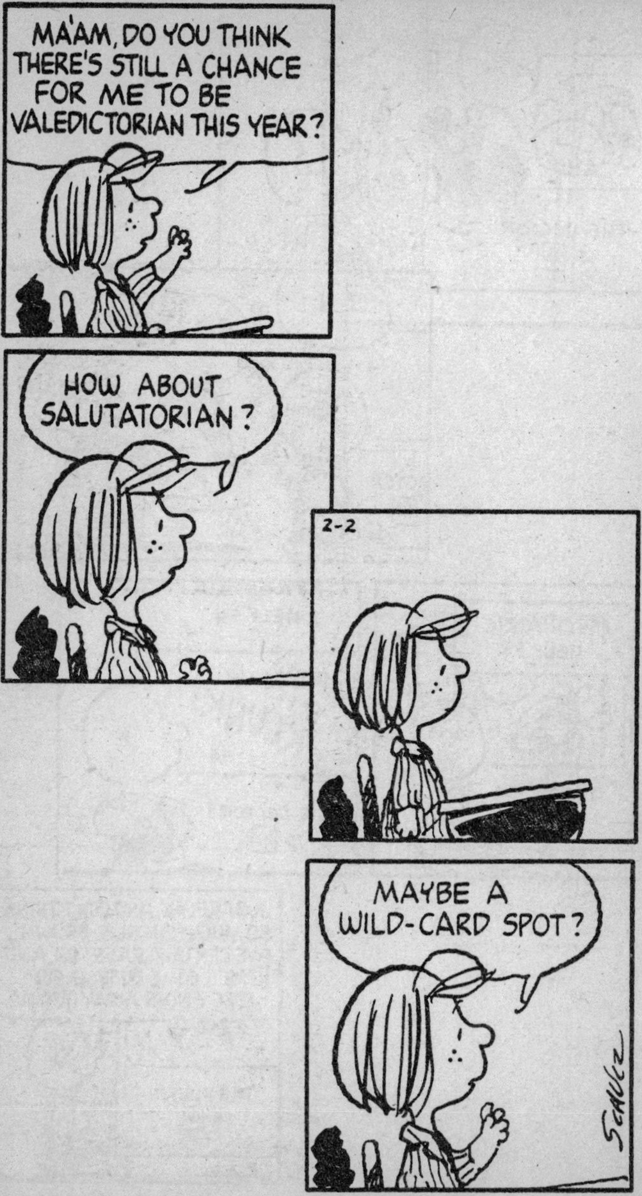
MA'AM, DO YOU THINK THERE'S STILL A CHANCE FOR ME TO BE VALEDICTORIAN THIS YEAR?
HOW ABOUT SALUTATORIAN?
2-2
MAYBE A WILD-CARD SPOT?
SCHULZ

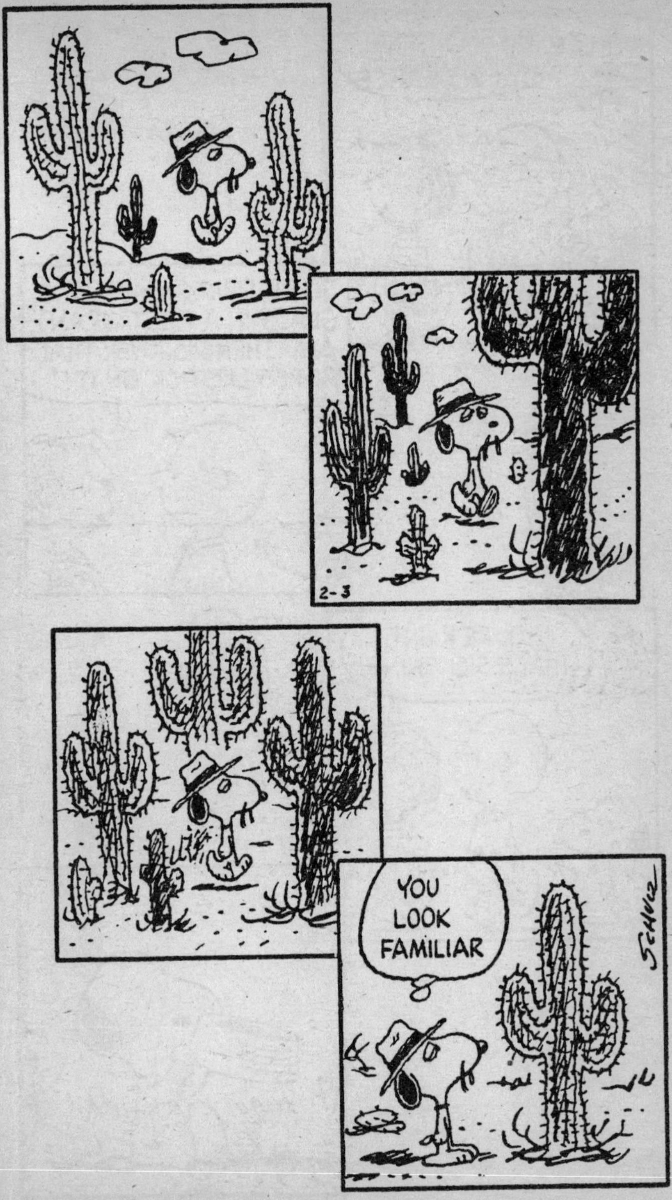
2-3
YOU LOOK FAMILIAR
SCHULZ

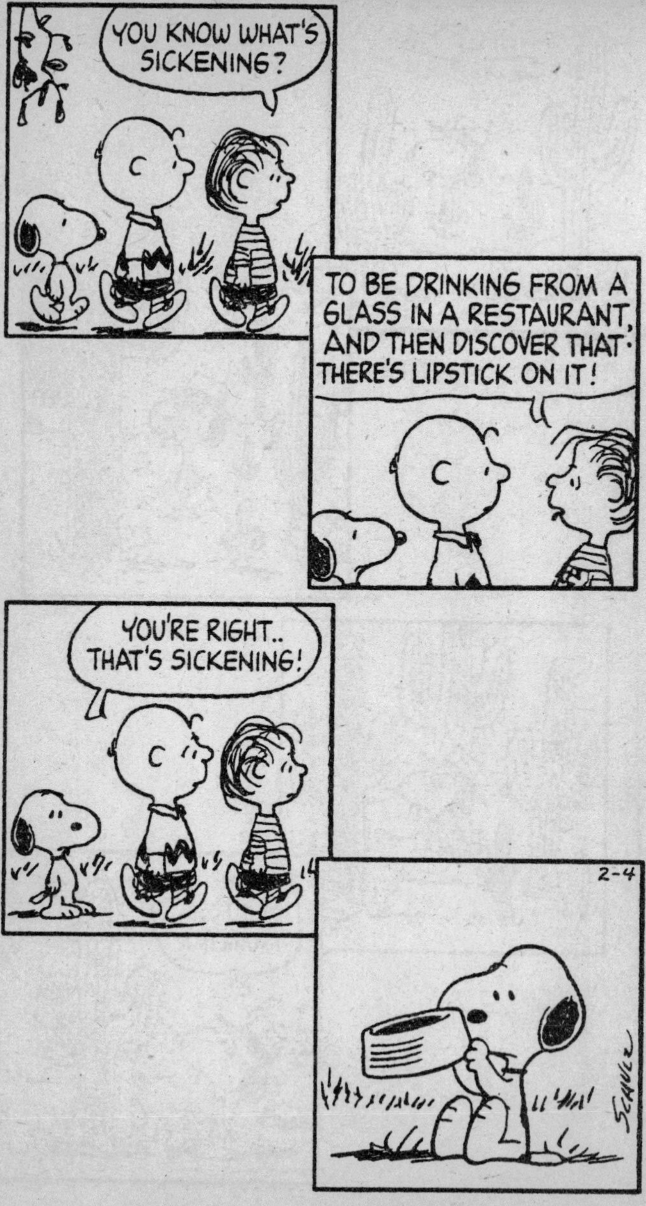
YOU KNOW WHAT'S SICKENING?
TO BE DRINKING FROM A GLASS IN A RESTAURANT, AND THEN DISCOVER THAT THERE'S LIPSTICK ON IT!
YOU'RE RIGHT.. THAT'S SICKENING!
2-4
SCHULZ

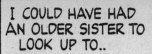

I COULD HAVE HAD AN OLDER SISTER TO LOOK UP TO..

OR I COULD HAVE HAD A YOUNGER SISTER WHO WOULD HAVE LOOKED UP TO ME...

INSTEAD, WHAT DID I GET?

I KNOW THE ANSWER!

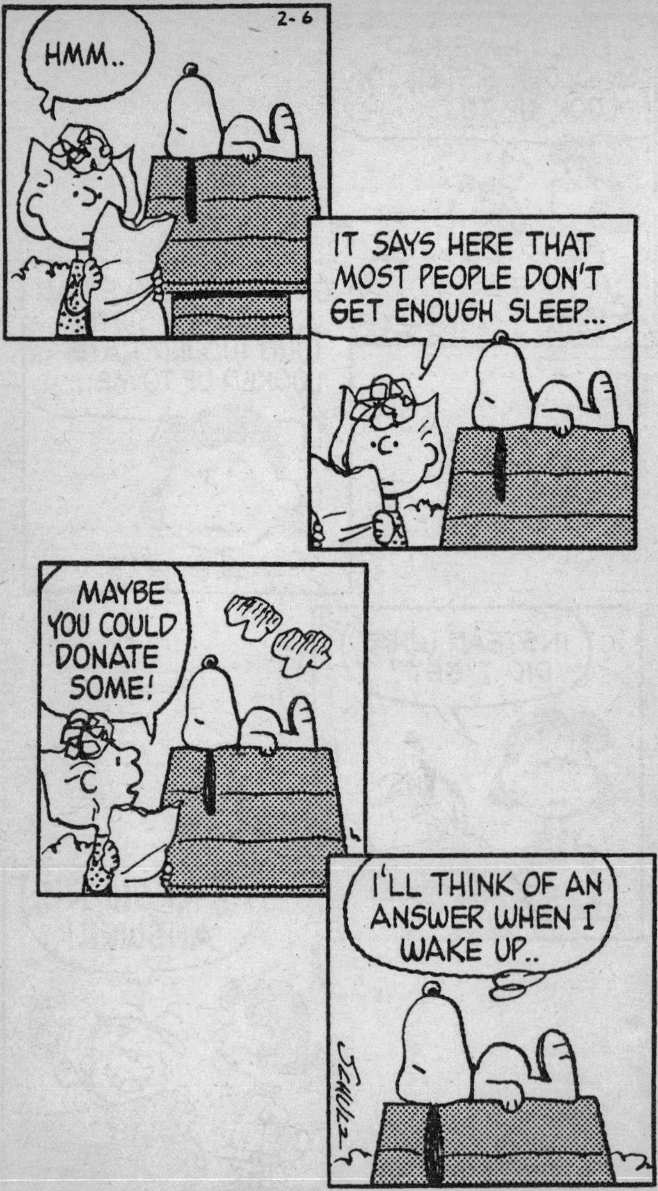
2-6
HMM..
IT SAYS HERE THAT MOST PEOPLE DON'T GET ENOUGH SLEEP...
MAYBE YOU COULD DONATE SOME!
I'LL THINK OF AN ANSWER WHEN I WAKE UP..
SCHULZ

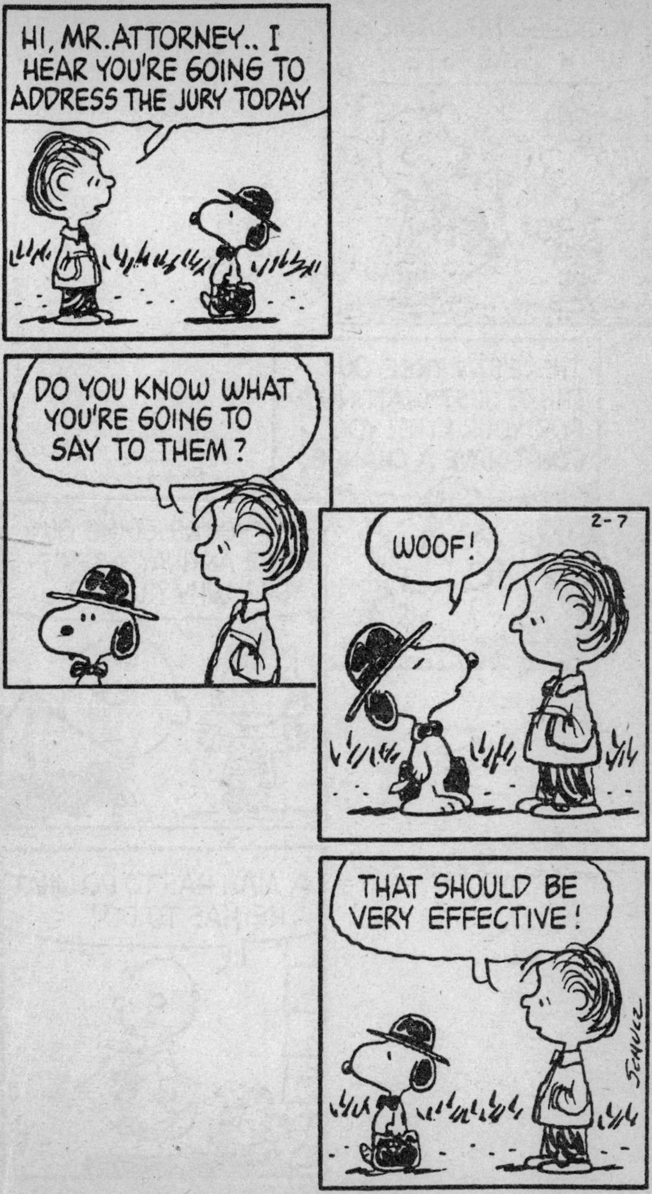
HI, MR. ATTORNEY.. I HEAR YOU'RE GOING TO ADDRESS THE JURY TODAY
DO YOU KNOW WHAT YOU'RE GOING TO SAY TO THEM?
2-7
WOOF!
THAT SHOULD BE VERY EFFECTIVE!
SCHULZ

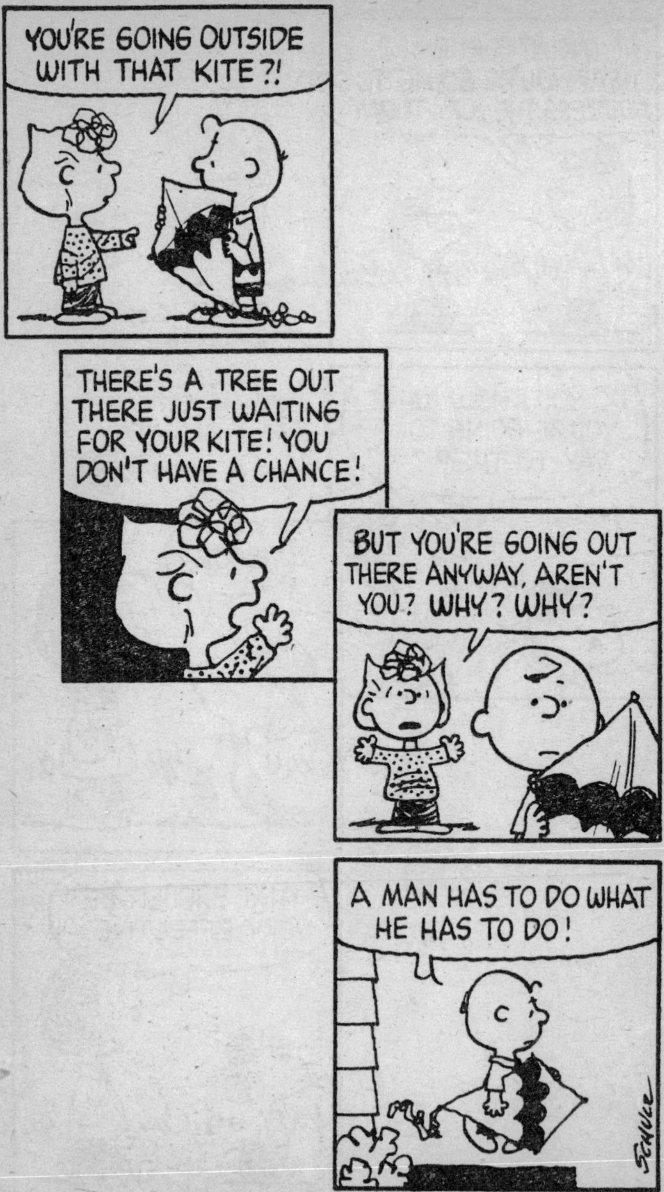
YOU'RE GOING OUTSIDE WITH THAT KITE?!
THERE'S A TREE OUT THERE JUST WAITING FOR YOUR KITE! YOU DON'T HAVE A CHANCE!
BUT YOU'RE GOING OUT THERE ANYWAY, AREN'T YOU? WHY? WHY?
A MAN HAS TO DO WHAT HE HAS TO DO!
SCHULZ

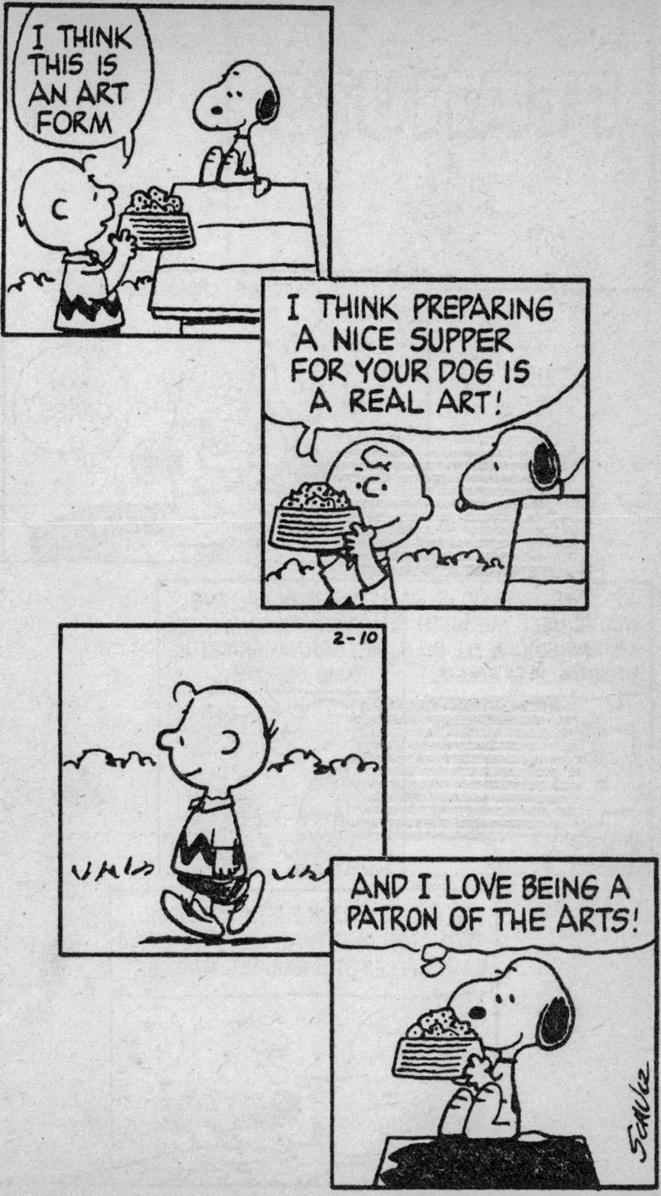
I THINK THIS IS AN ART FORM
I THINK PREPARING A NICE SUPPER FOR YOUR DOG IS A REAL ART!
2-10
AND I LOVE BEING A PATRON OF THE ARTS!
SCHULZ

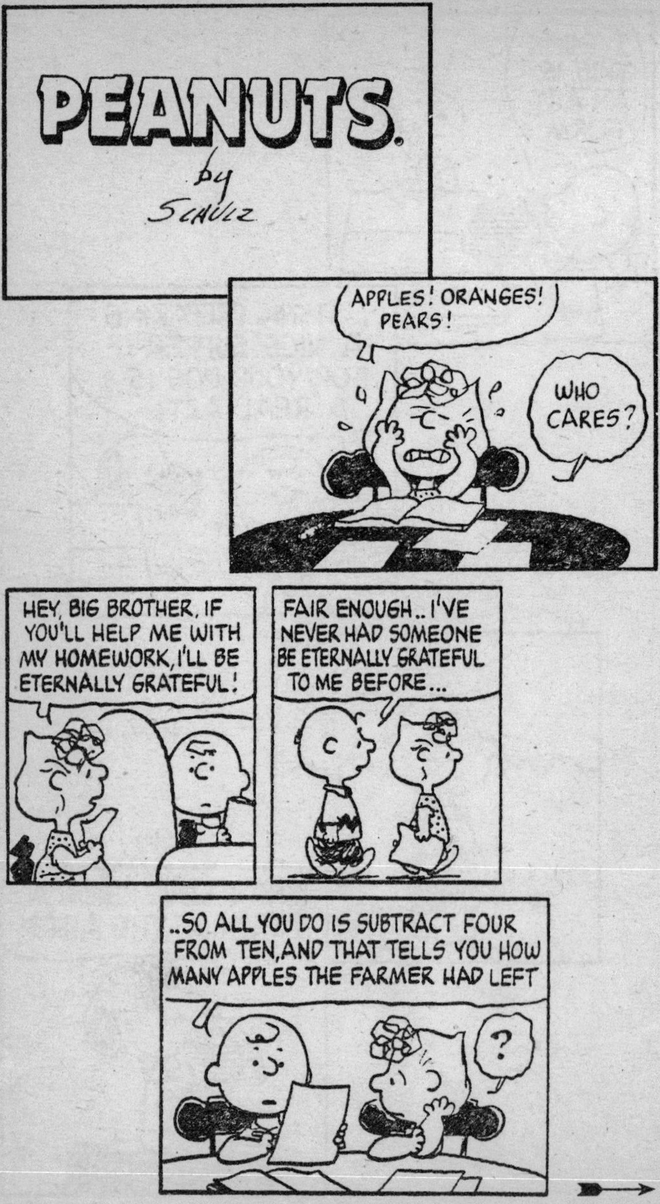
PEANUTS
by SCHULZ
APPLES! ORANGES! PEARS!
WHO CARES?
HEY, BIG BROTHER, IF YOU'LL HELP ME WITH MY HOMEWORK, I'LL BE ETERNALLY GRATEFUL!
FAIR ENOUGH.. I'VE NEVER HAD SOMEONE BE ETERNALLY GRATEFUL TO ME BEFORE...
..SO ALL YOU DO IS SUBTRACT FOUR FROM TEN, AND THAT TELLS YOU HOW MANY APPLES THE FARMER HAD LEFT
?

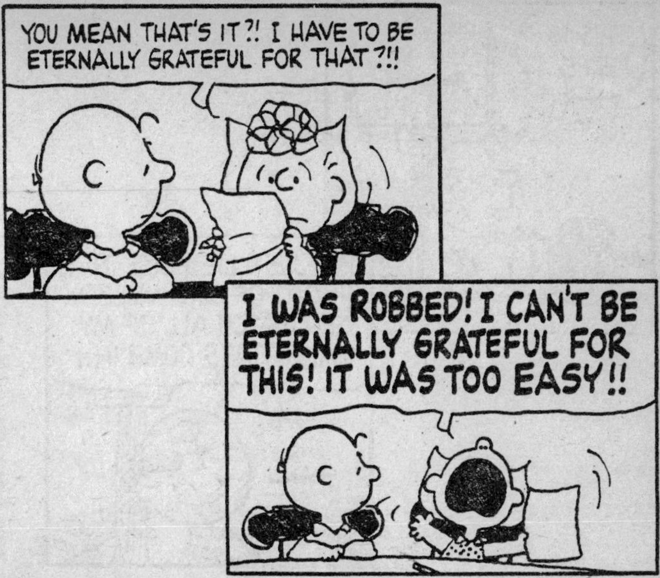
YOU MEAN THAT'S IT?! I HAVE TO BE ETERNALLY GRATEFUL FOR THAT?!!
I WAS ROBBED! I CAN'T BE ETERNALLY GRATEFUL FOR THIS! IT WAS TOO EASY!!

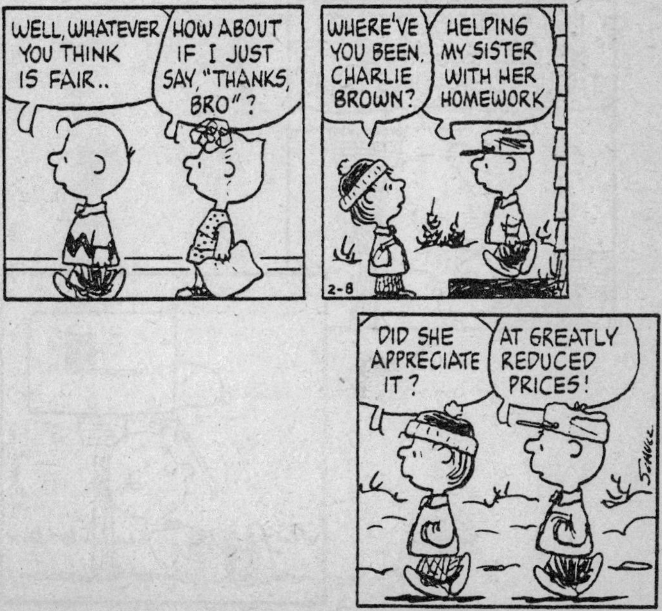
WELL, WHATEVER YOU THINK IS FAIR..
HOW ABOUT IF I JUST SAY, "THANKS, BRO"?
WHERE'VE YOU BEEN, CHARLIE BROWN?
HELPING MY SISTER WITH HER HOMEWORK
2-8
DID SHE APPRECIATE IT?
AT GREATLY REDUCED PRICES!

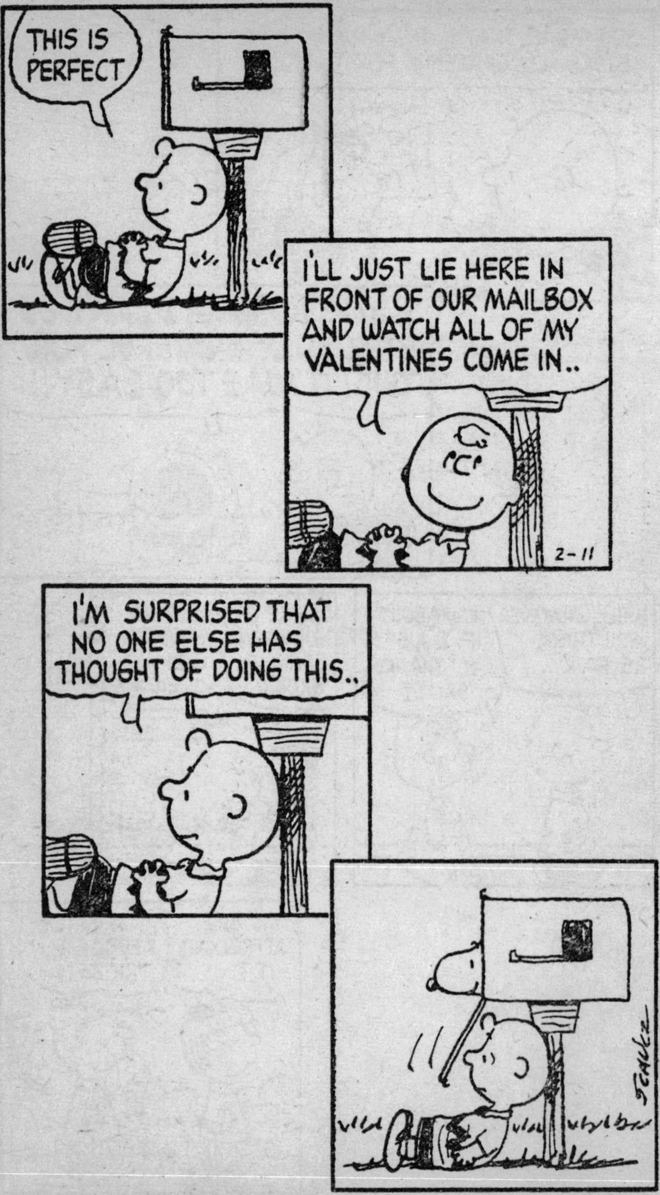
THIS IS PERFECT
I'LL JUST LIE HERE IN FRONT OF OUR MAILBOX AND WATCH ALL OF MY VALENTINES COME IN..
2-11
I'M SURPRISED THAT NO ONE ELSE HAS THOUGHT OF DOING THIS..
SCHULZ

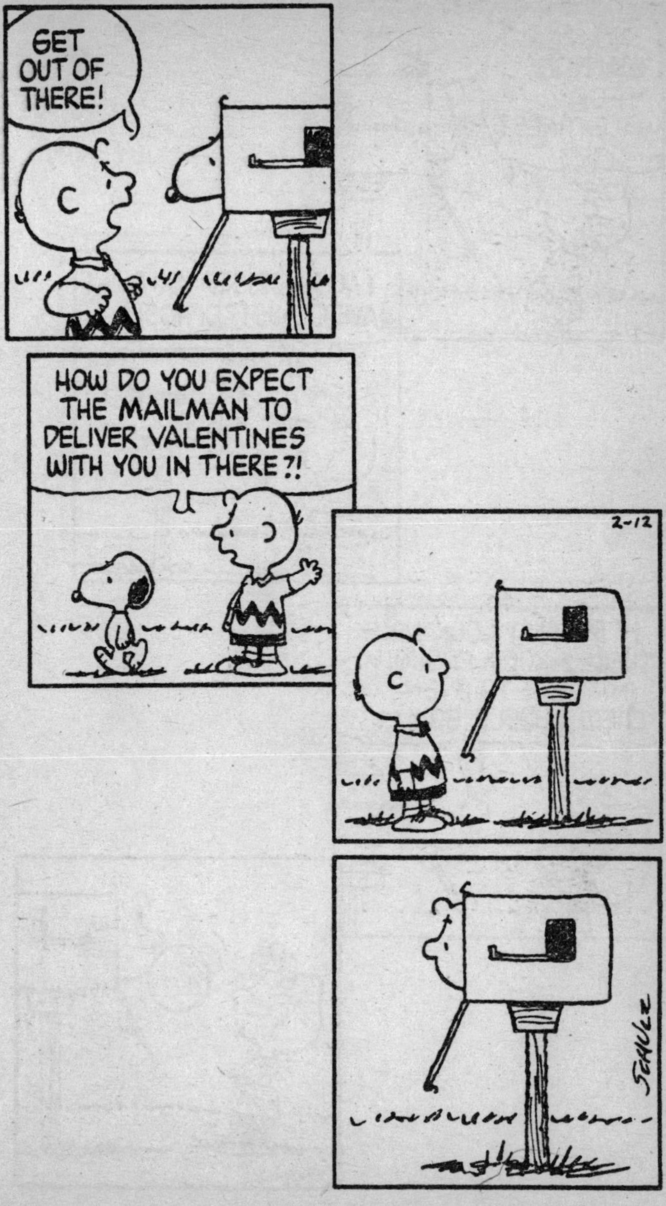
GET OUT OF THERE!
HOW DO YOU EXPECT THE MAILMAN TO DELIVER VALENTINES WITH YOU IN THERE?!
2-12
SCHULZ

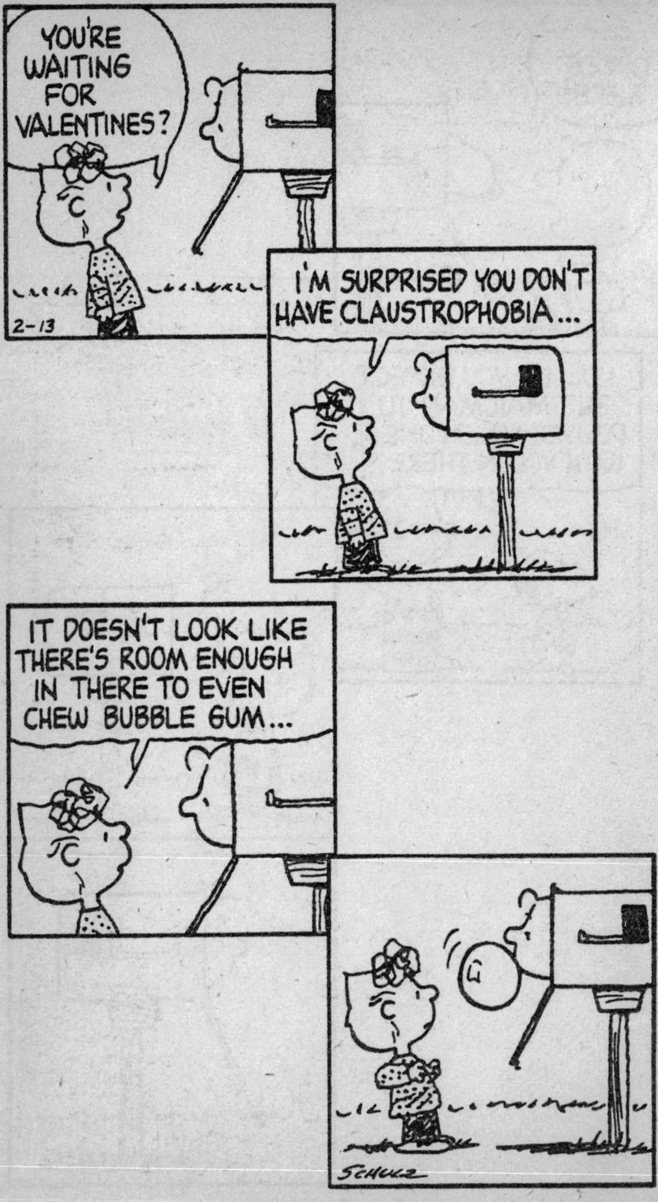
YOU'RE WAITING FOR VALENTINES?
2-13
I'M SURPRISED YOU DON'T HAVE CLAUSTROPHOBIA...
IT DOESN'T LOOK LIKE THERE'S ROOM ENOUGH IN THERE TO EVEN CHEW BUBBLE GUM...
SCHULZ

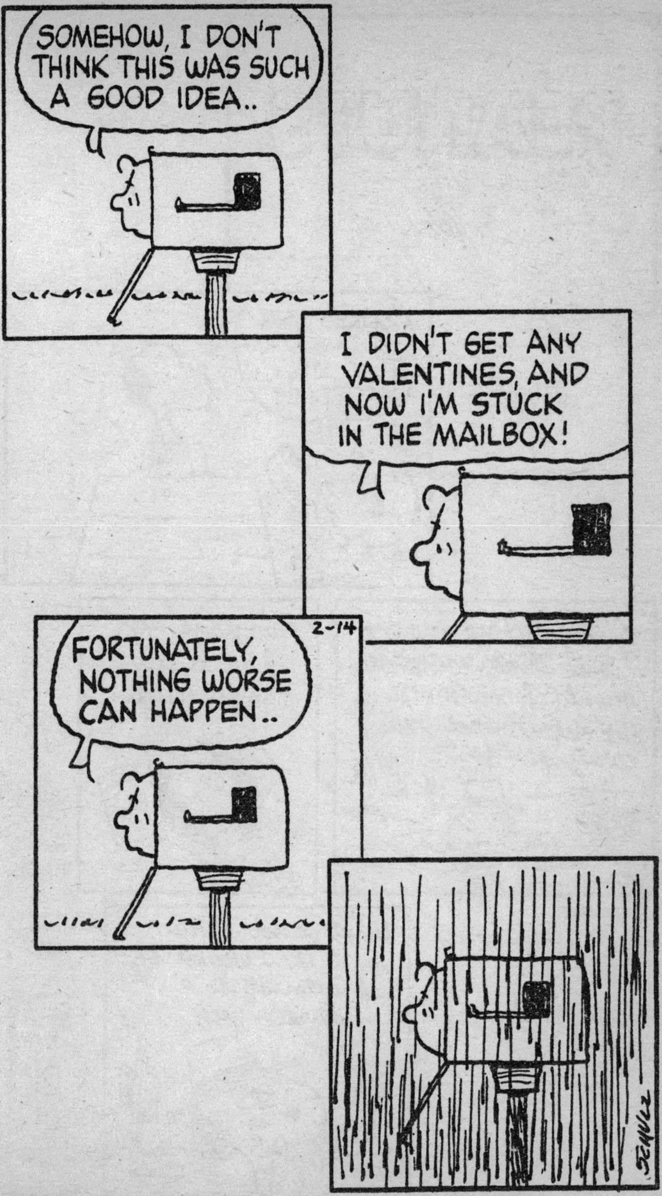
SOMEHOW, I DON'T THINK THIS WAS SUCH A GOOD IDEA..
I DIDN'T GET ANY VALENTINES, AND NOW I'M STUCK IN THE MAILBOX!
2-14
FORTUNATELY, NOTHING WORSE CAN HAPPEN..
SCHULZ

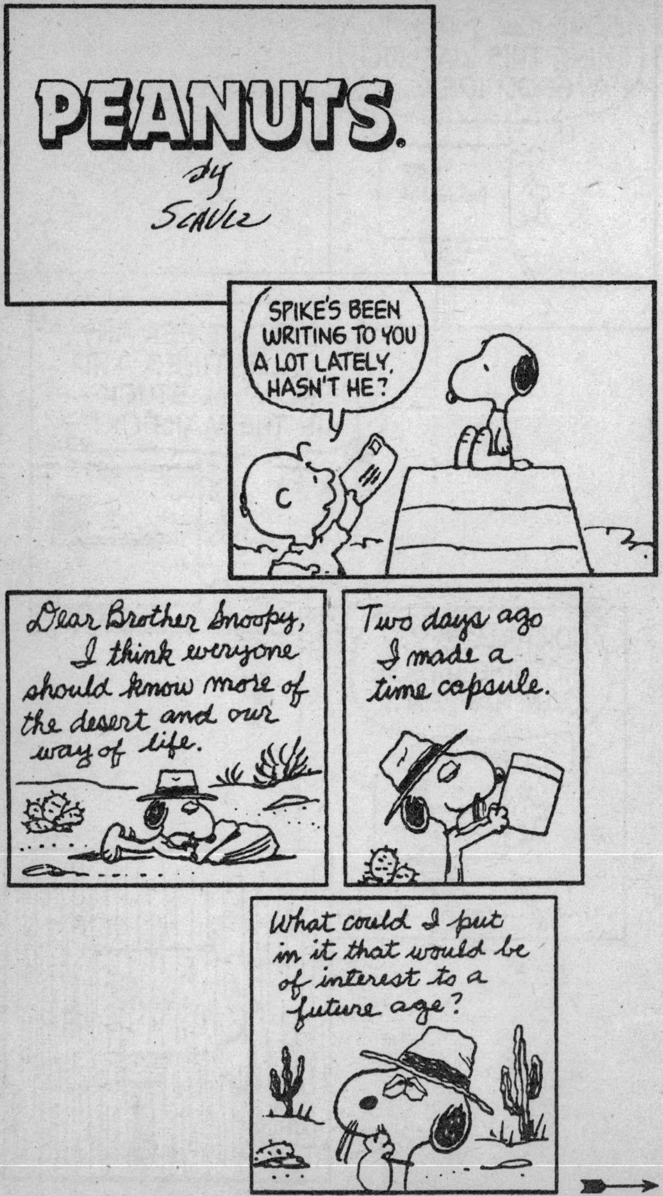
PEANUTS.
by Schulz
SPIKE'S BEEN WRITING TO YOU A LOT LATELY, HASN'T HE?
Dear Brother Snoopy, I think everyone should know more of the desert and our way of life.
Two days ago I made a time capsule.
What could I put in it that would be of interest to a future age?

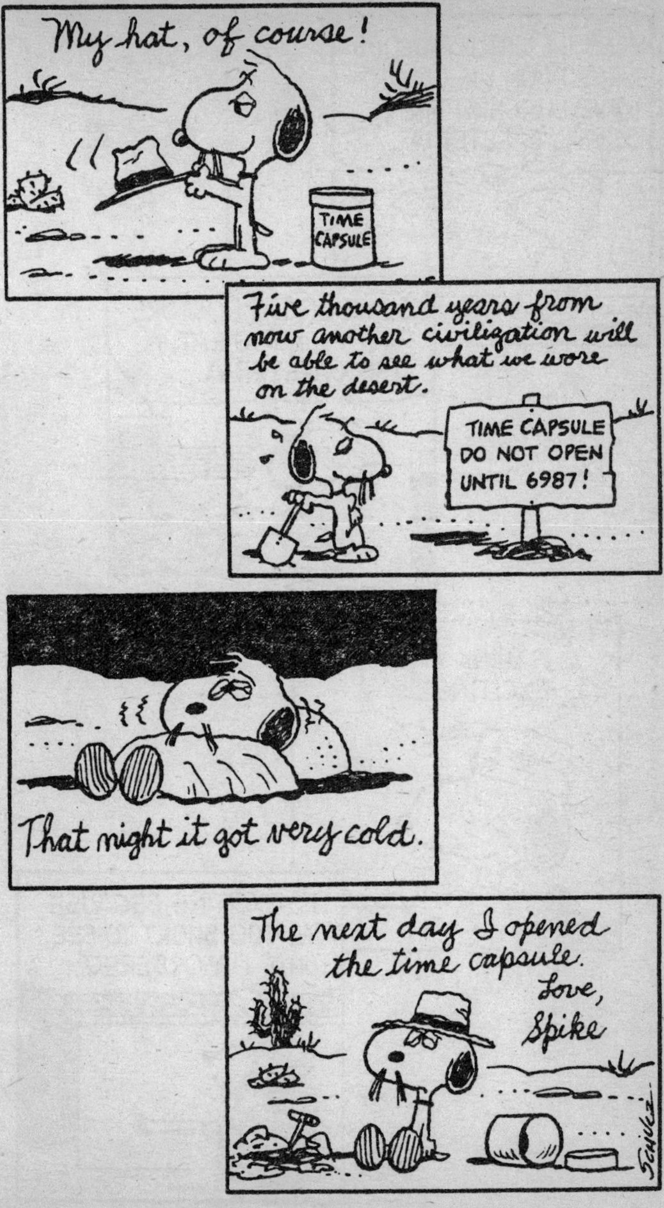
My hat, of course!
TIME CAPSULE
Five thousand years from now another civilization will be able to see what we wore on the desert.
TIME CAPSULE DO NOT OPEN UNTIL 6987!
That night it got very cold.
The next day I opened the time capsule.
Love, Spike

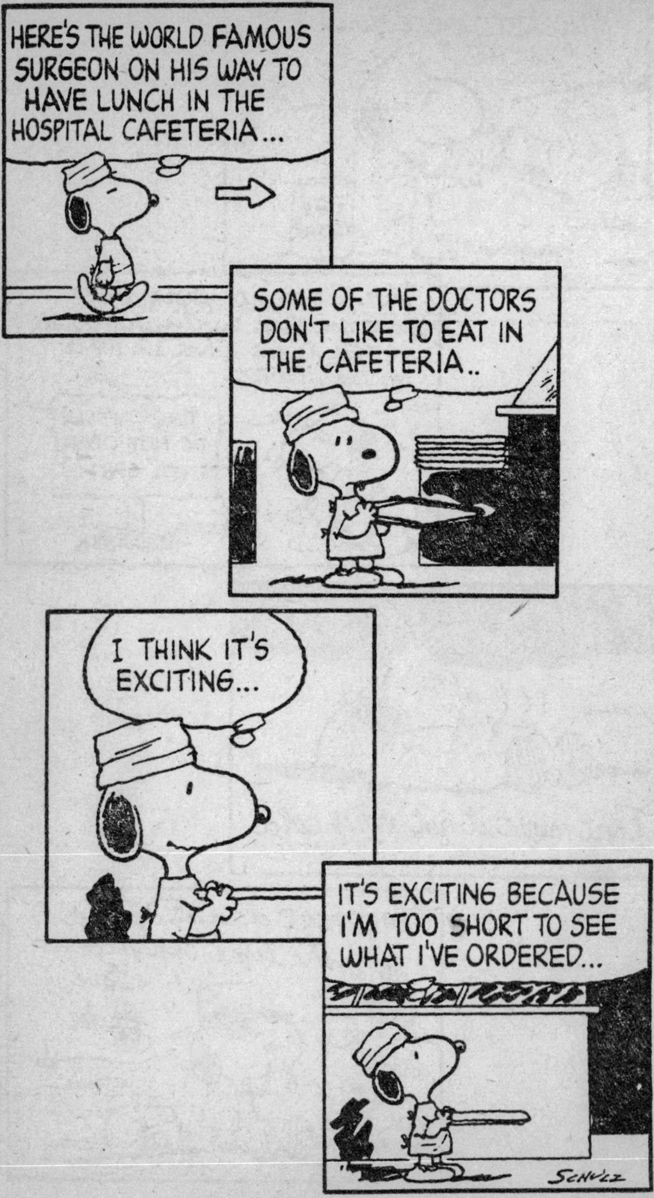
HERE'S THE WORLD FAMOUS SURGEON ON HIS WAY TO HAVE LUNCH IN THE HOSPITAL CAFETERIA...
SOME OF THE DOCTORS DON'T LIKE TO EAT IN THE CAFETERIA..
I THINK IT'S EXCITING...
IT'S EXCITING BECAUSE I'M TOO SHORT TO SEE WHAT I'VE ORDERED...
SCHULZ

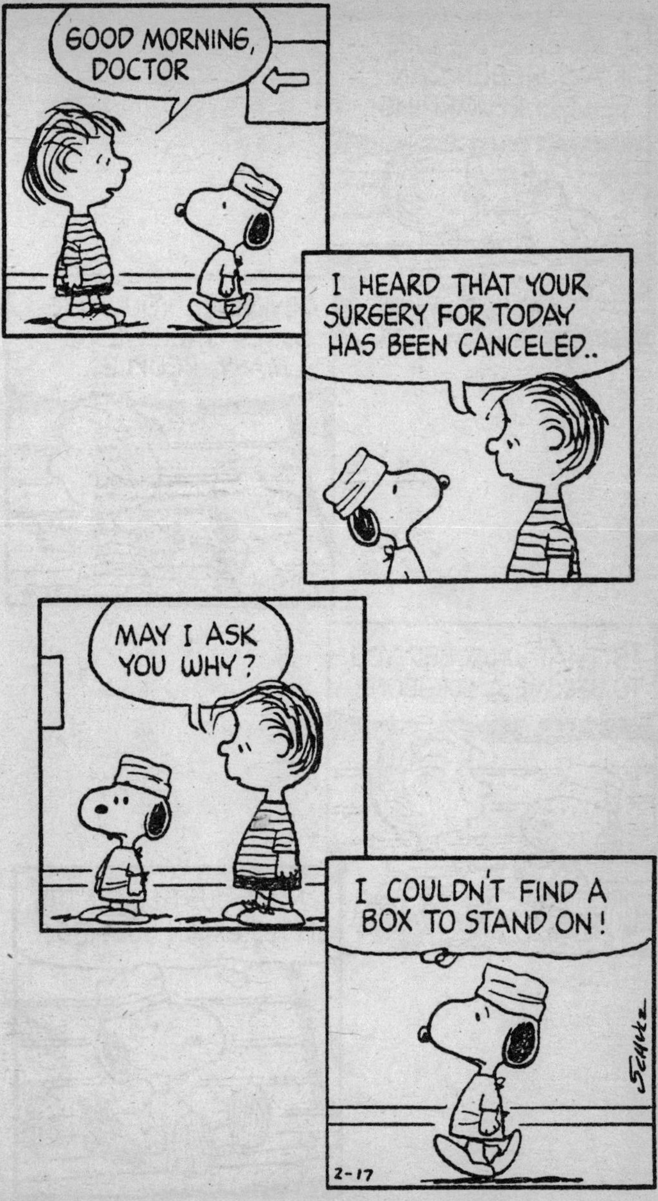
GOOD MORNING, DOCTOR
I HEARD THAT YOUR SURGERY FOR TODAY HAS BEEN CANCELED..
MAY I ASK YOU WHY?
I COULDN'T FIND A BOX TO STAND ON!
SCHULZ
2-17

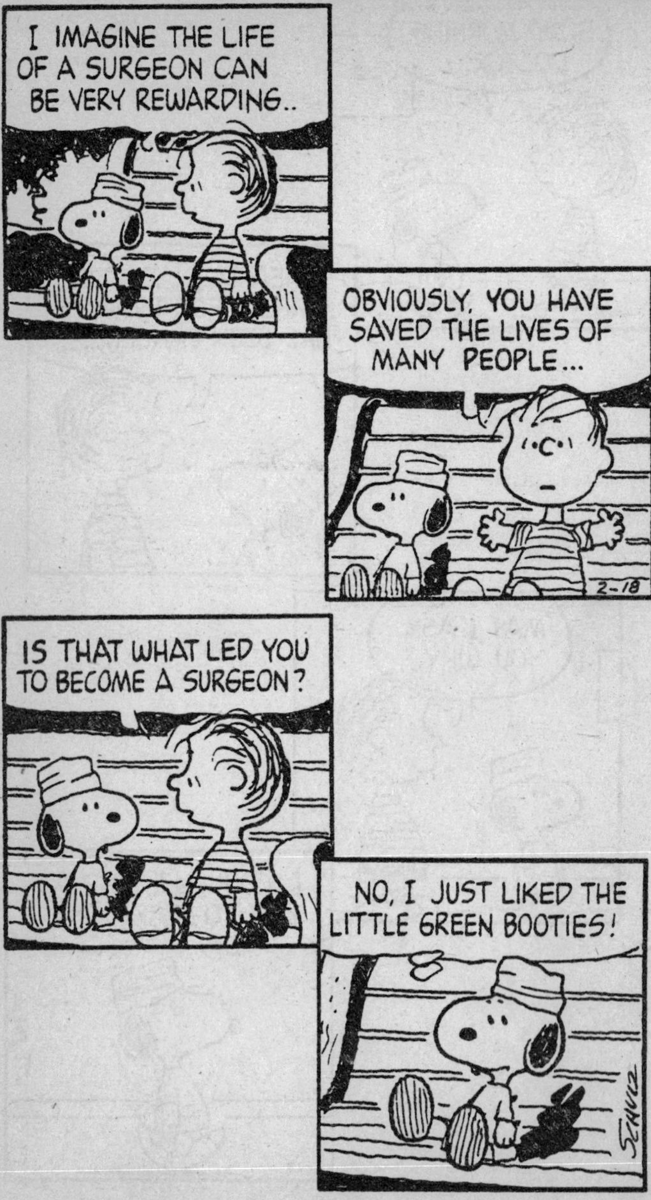
I IMAGINE THE LIFE OF A SURGEON CAN BE VERY REWARDING..
OBVIOUSLY, YOU HAVE SAVED THE LIVES OF MANY PEOPLE...
2-18
IS THAT WHAT LED YOU TO BECOME A SURGEON?
NO, I JUST LIKED THE LITTLE GREEN BOOTIES!

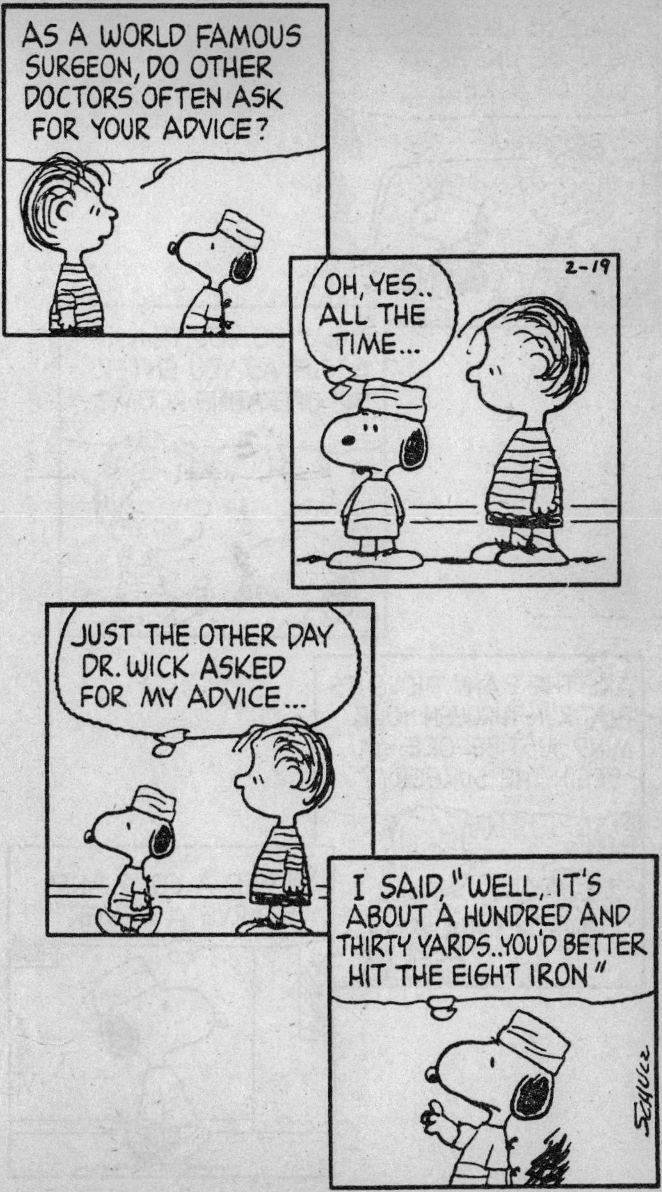
AS A WORLD FAMOUS SURGEON, DO OTHER DOCTORS OFTEN ASK FOR YOUR ADVICE?
2-19
OH, YES.. ALL THE TIME...
JUST THE OTHER DAY DR. WICK ASKED FOR MY ADVICE...
I SAID, "WELL, IT'S ABOUT A HUNDRED AND THIRTY YARDS..YOU'D BETTER HIT THE EIGHT IRON"
SCHULZ

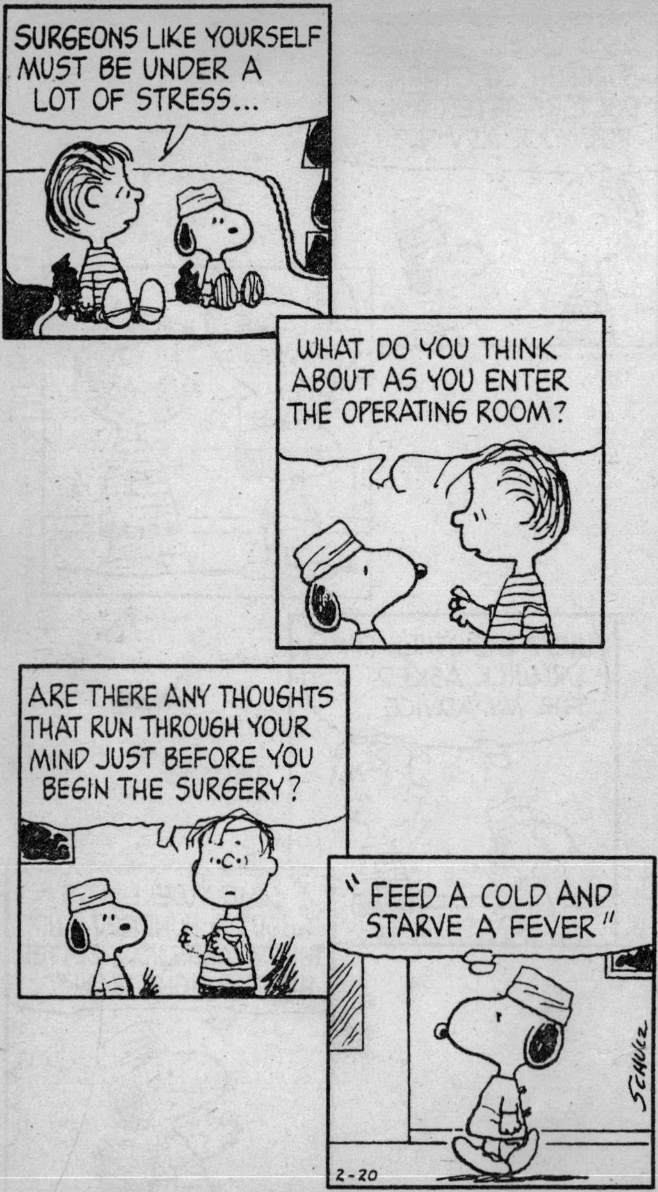
SURGEONS LIKE YOURSELF MUST BE UNDER A LOT OF STRESS...
WHAT DO YOU THINK ABOUT AS YOU ENTER THE OPERATING ROOM?
ARE THERE ANY THOUGHTS THAT RUN THROUGH YOUR MIND JUST BEFORE YOU BEGIN THE SURGERY?
"FEED A COLD AND STARVE A FEVER"
SCHULZ
2-20

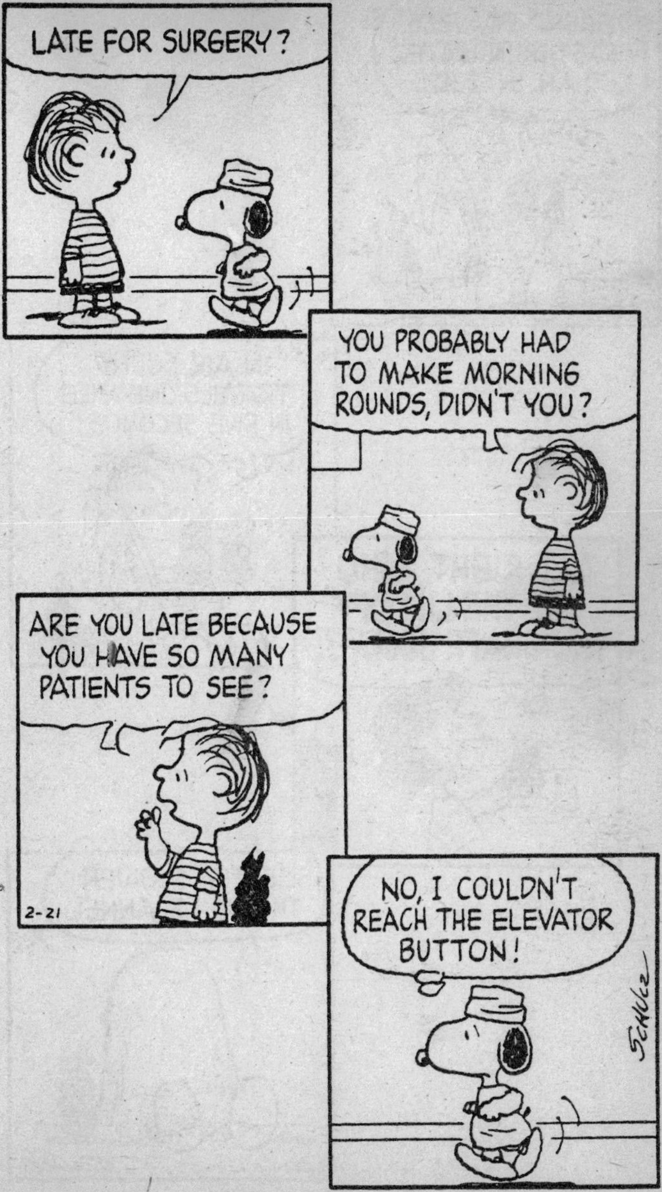
LATE FOR SURGERY?
YOU PROBABLY HAD TO MAKE MORNING ROUNDS, DIDN'T YOU?
ARE YOU LATE BECAUSE YOU HAVE SO MANY PATIENTS TO SEE?
2-21
NO, I COULDN'T REACH THE ELEVATOR BUTTON!
SCHULZ

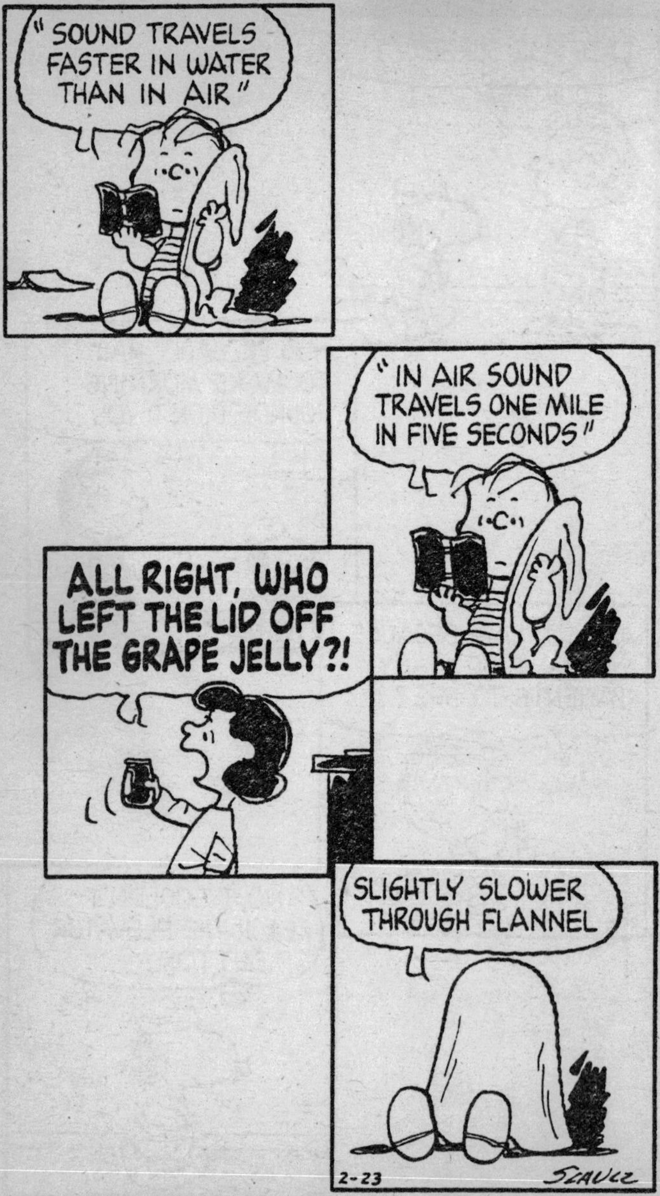
"SOUND TRAVELS FASTER IN WATER THAN IN AIR"
"IN AIR SOUND TRAVELS ONE MILE IN FIVE SECONDS"
ALL RIGHT, WHO LEFT THE LID OFF THE GRAPE JELLY?!
SLIGHTLY SLOWER THROUGH FLANNEL
2-23
SCHULZ

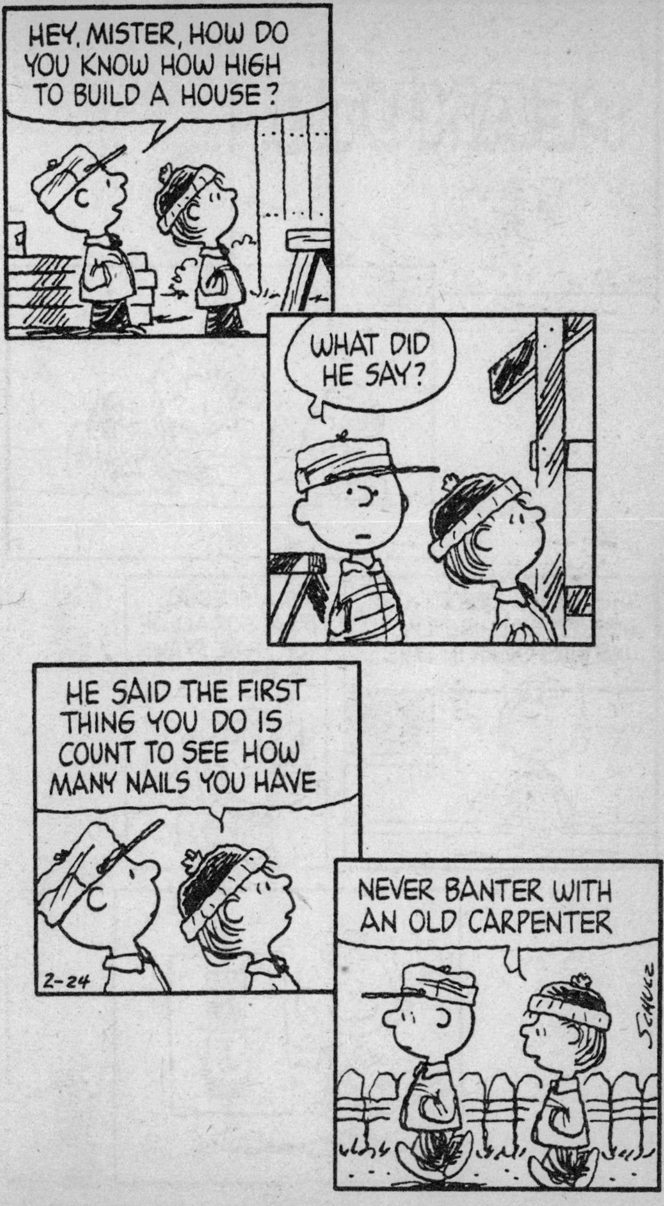
HEY, MISTER, HOW DO YOU KNOW HOW HIGH TO BUILD A HOUSE?
WHAT DID HE SAY?
HE SAID THE FIRST THING YOU DO IS COUNT TO SEE HOW MANY NAILS YOU HAVE
2-24
NEVER BANTER WITH AN OLD CARPENTER
SCHULZ

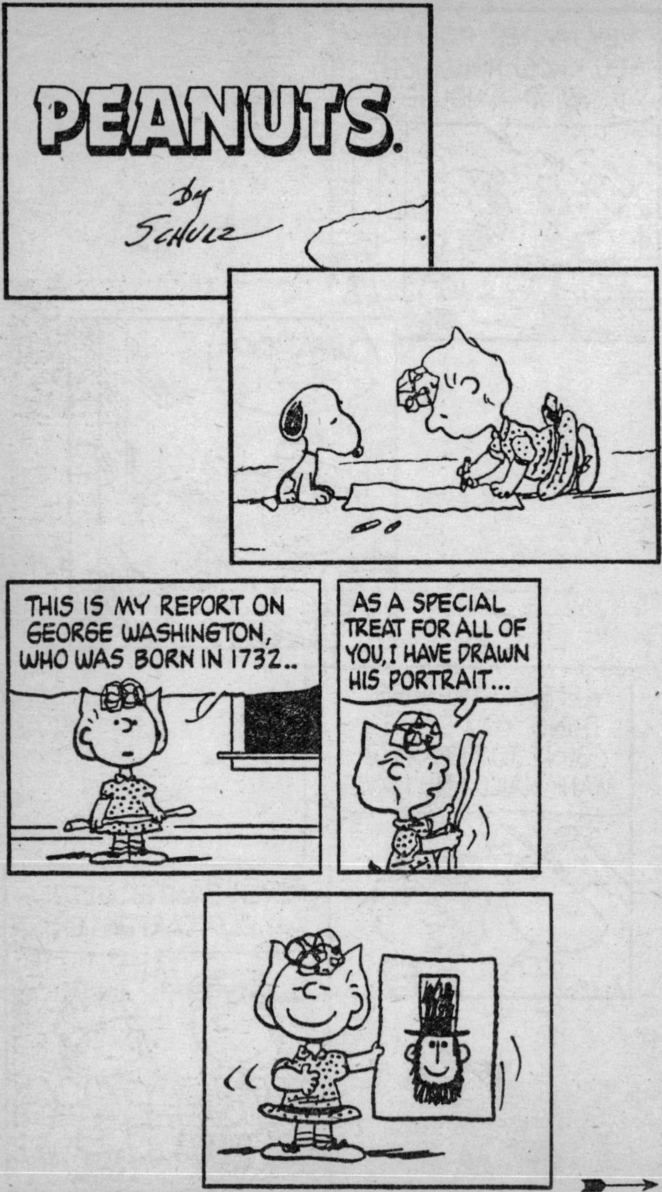
PEANUTS
by SCHULZ
THIS IS MY REPORT ON GEORGE WASHINGTON, WHO WAS BORN IN 1732...
AS A SPECIAL TREAT FOR ALL OF YOU, I HAVE DRAWN HIS PORTRAIT...

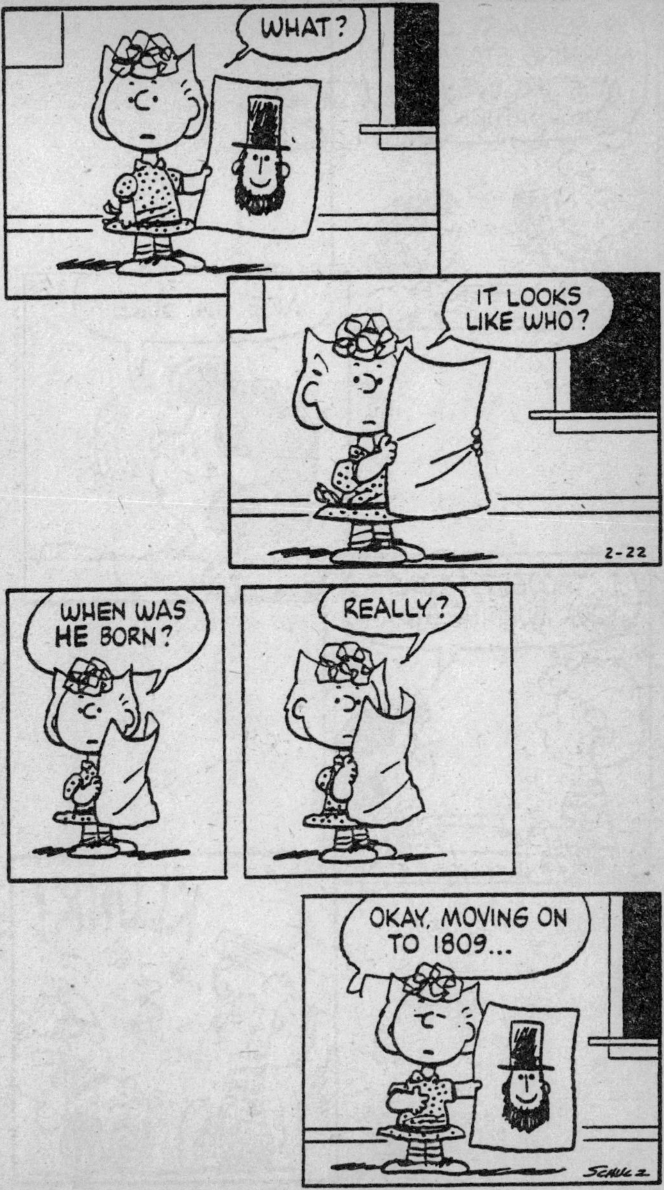
WHAT?
IT LOOKS LIKE WHO?
2-22
WHEN WAS HE BORN?
REALLY?
OKAY, MOVING ON TO 1809...
SCHULZ

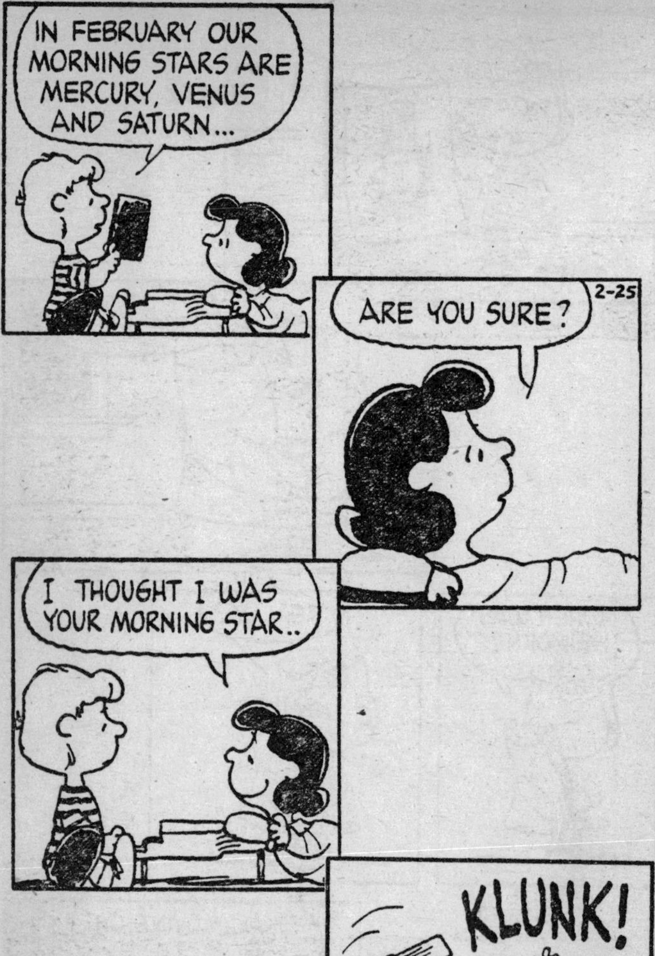
IN FEBRUARY OUR MORNING STARS ARE MERCURY, VENUS AND SATURN...
2-25
ARE YOU SURE?
I THOUGHT I WAS YOUR MORNING STAR..
KLUNK!
SCHULZ

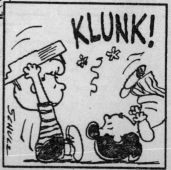

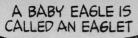

A BABY EAGLE IS CALLED AN EAGLET

A KANGAROO IS A JOEY.. A CODFISH IS A CODLING...

WHAT DO THEY CALL A BABY BROTHER?

PATHETIC!

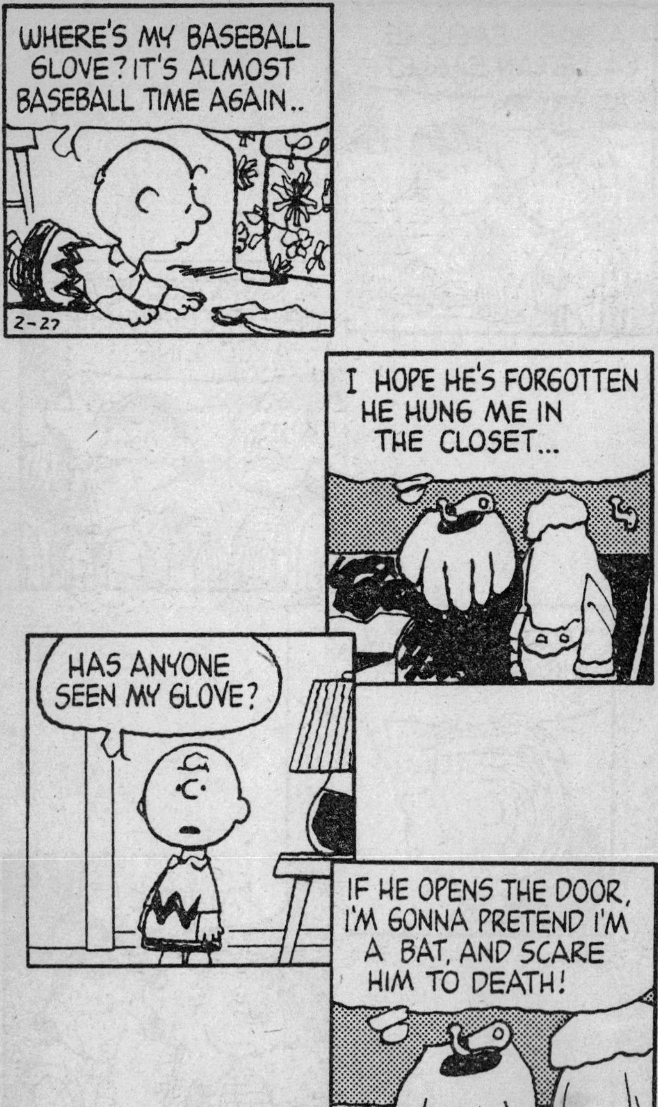
WHERE'S MY BASEBALL GLOVE? IT'S ALMOST BASEBALL TIME AGAIN..
2-27
I HOPE HE'S FORGOTTEN HE HUNG ME IN THE CLOSET...
HAS ANYONE SEEN MY GLOVE?
IF HE OPENS THE DOOR, I'M GONNA PRETEND I'M A BAT, AND SCARE HIM TO DEATH!
SCHULZ

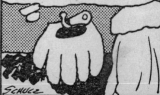

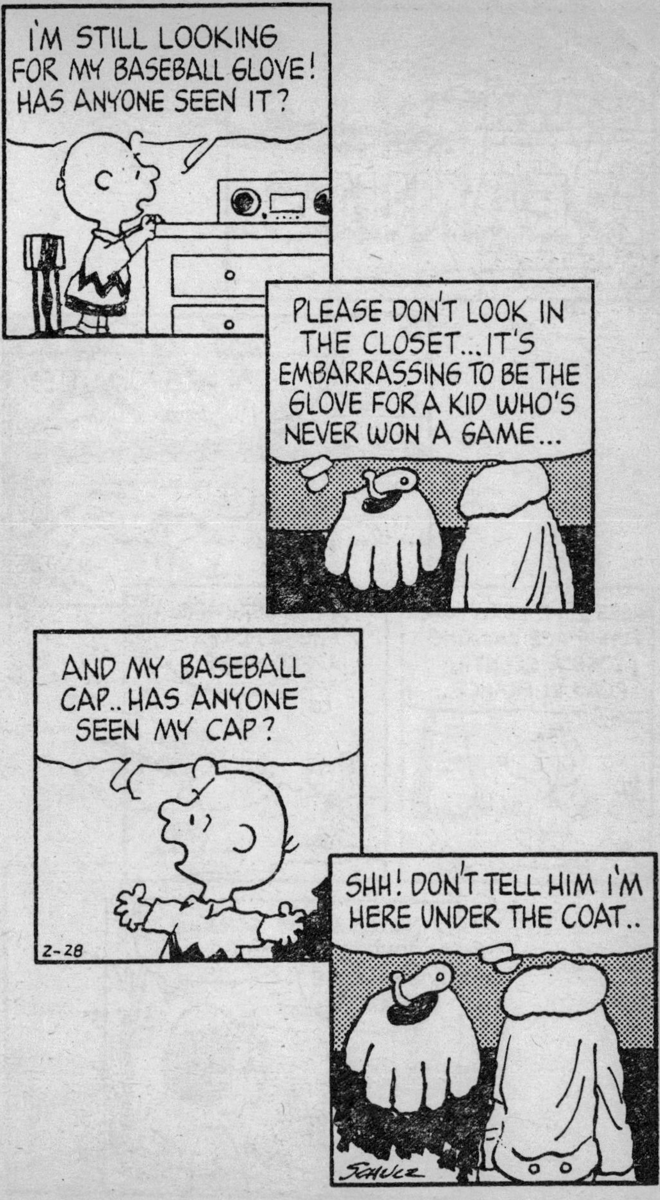
I'M STILL LOOKING FOR MY BASEBALL GLOVE! HAS ANYONE SEEN IT?
PLEASE DON'T LOOK IN THE CLOSET...IT'S EMBARRASSING TO BE THE GLOVE FOR A KID WHO'S NEVER WON A GAME...
AND MY BASEBALL CAP.. HAS ANYONE SEEN MY CAP?
2-28
SHH! DON'T TELL HIM I'M HERE UNDER THE COAT..
SCHULZ

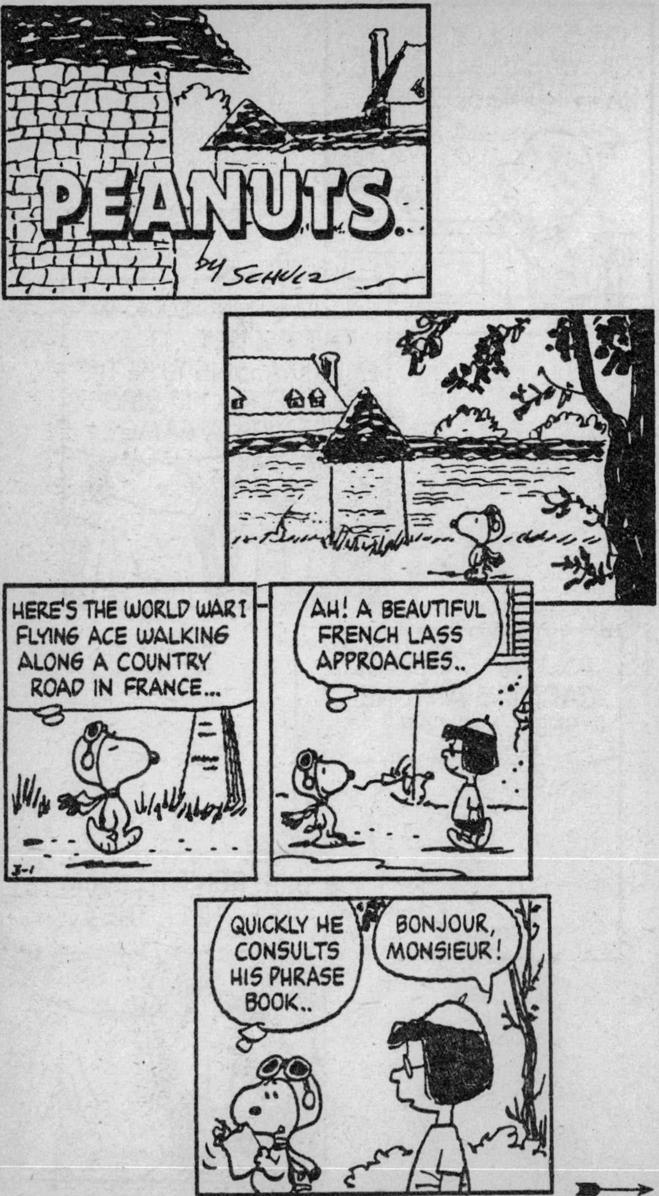

PEANUTS
by SCHULZ
HERE'S THE WORLD WAR I FLYING ACE WALKING ALONG A COUNTRY ROAD IN FRANCE...
3-1
AH! A BEAUTIFUL FRENCH LASS APPROACHES..
QUICKLY HE CONSULTS HIS PHRASE BOOK..
BONJOUR, MONSIEUR!

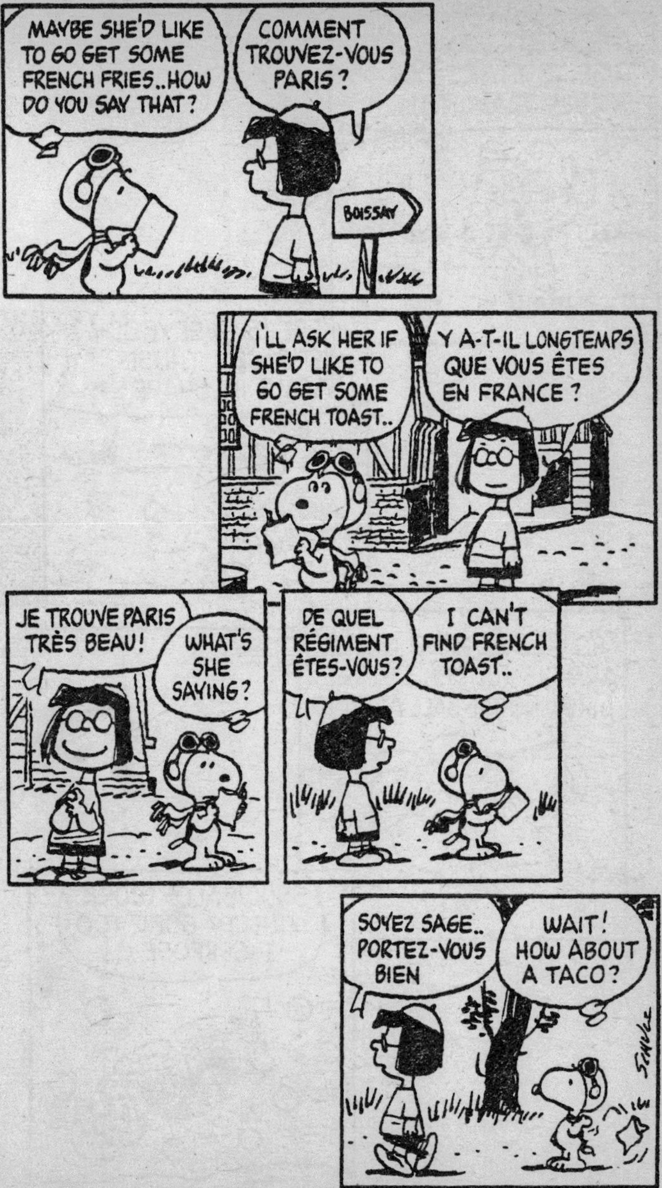

MAYBE SHE'D LIKE TO GO GET SOME FRENCH FRIES..HOW DO YOU SAY THAT?
COMMENT TROUVEZ-VOUS PARIS?
BOISSAY
I'LL ASK HER IF SHE'D LIKE TO GO GET SOME FRENCH TOAST..
Y A-T-IL LONGTEMPS QUE VOUS ÊTES EN FRANCE?
JE TROUVE PARIS TRÈS BEAU!
WHAT'S SHE SAYING?
DE QUEL RÉGIMENT ÊTES-VOUS?
I CAN'T FIND FRENCH TOAST..
SOYEZ SAGE.. PORTEZ-VOUS BIEN
WAIT! HOW ABOUT A TACO?

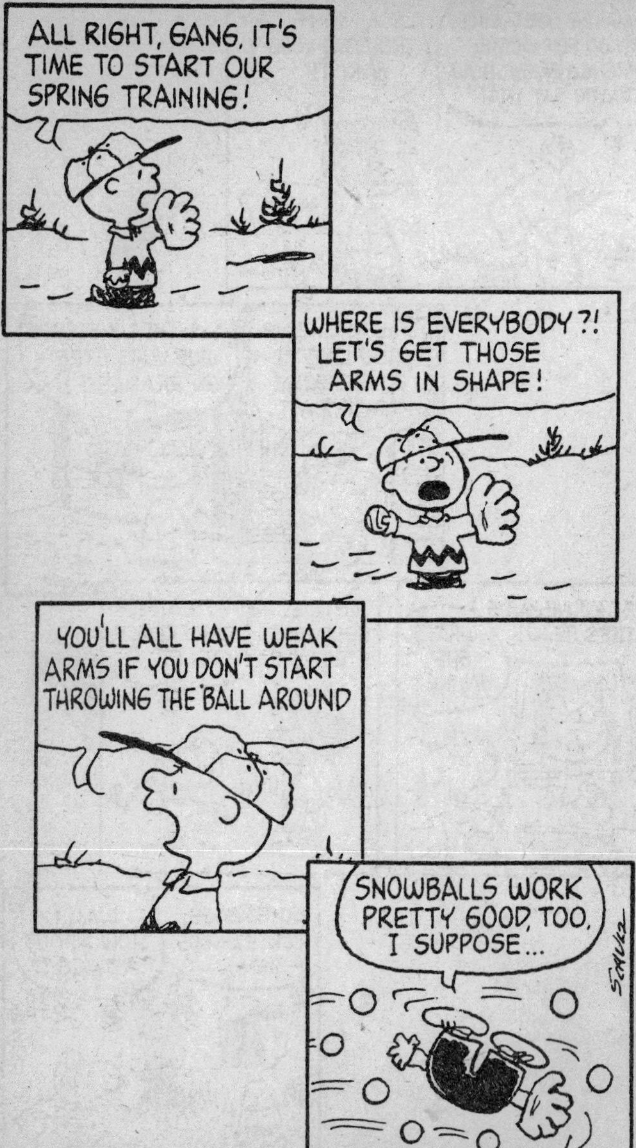
ALL RIGHT, GANG, IT'S TIME TO START OUR SPRING TRAINING!
WHERE IS EVERYBODY?! LET'S GET THOSE ARMS IN SHAPE!
YOU'LL ALL HAVE WEAK ARMS IF YOU DON'T START THROWING THE BALL AROUND
SNOWBALLS WORK PRETTY GOOD, TOO, I SUPPOSE...
SCHULZ

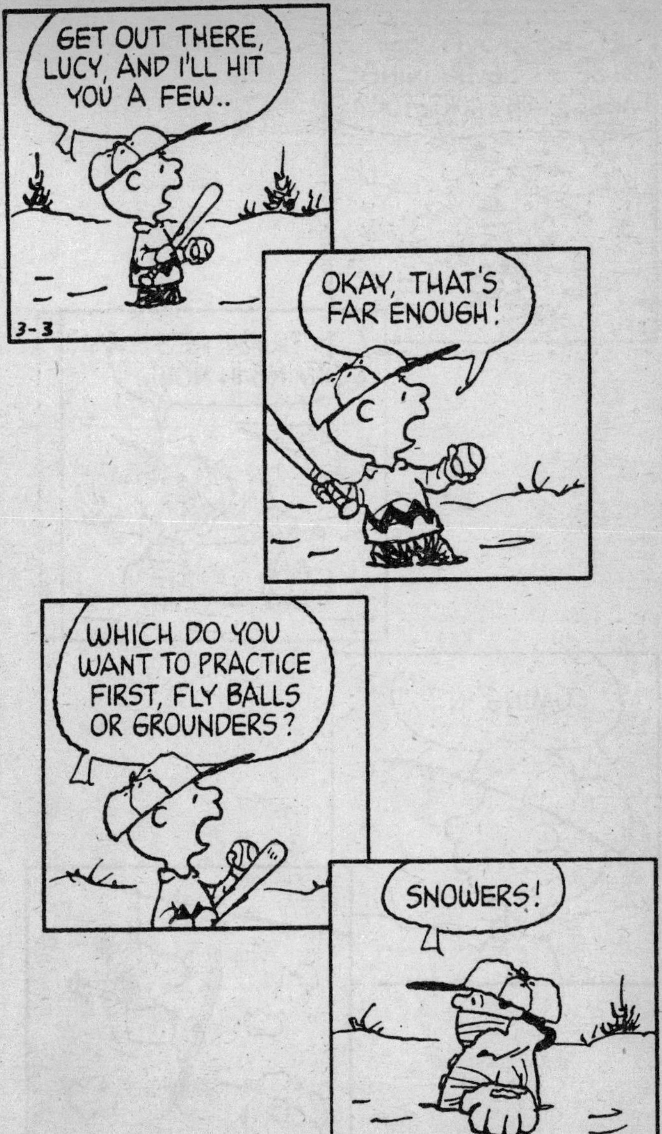
GET OUT THERE, LUCY, AND I'LL HIT YOU A FEW..
3-3
OKAY, THAT'S FAR ENOUGH!
WHICH DO YOU WANT TO PRACTICE FIRST, FLY BALLS OR GROUNDERS?
SNOWERS!
SCHULZ

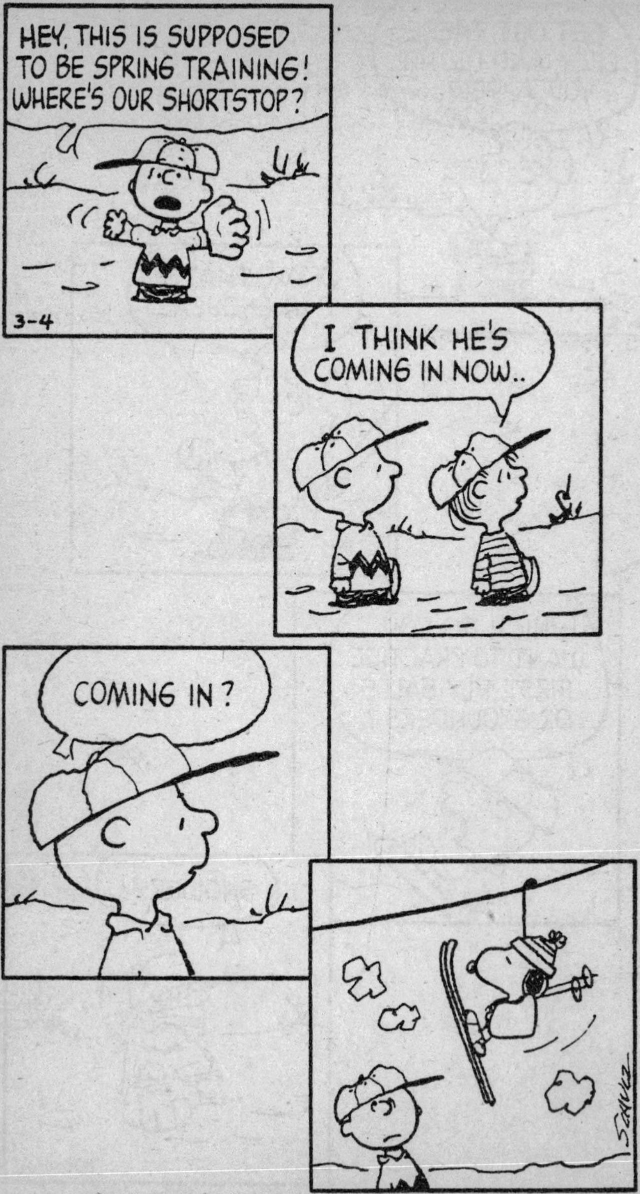
HEY, THIS IS SUPPOSED TO BE SPRING TRAINING! WHERE'S OUR SHORTSTOP?
3-4
I THINK HE'S COMING IN NOW..
COMING IN?
SCHULZ

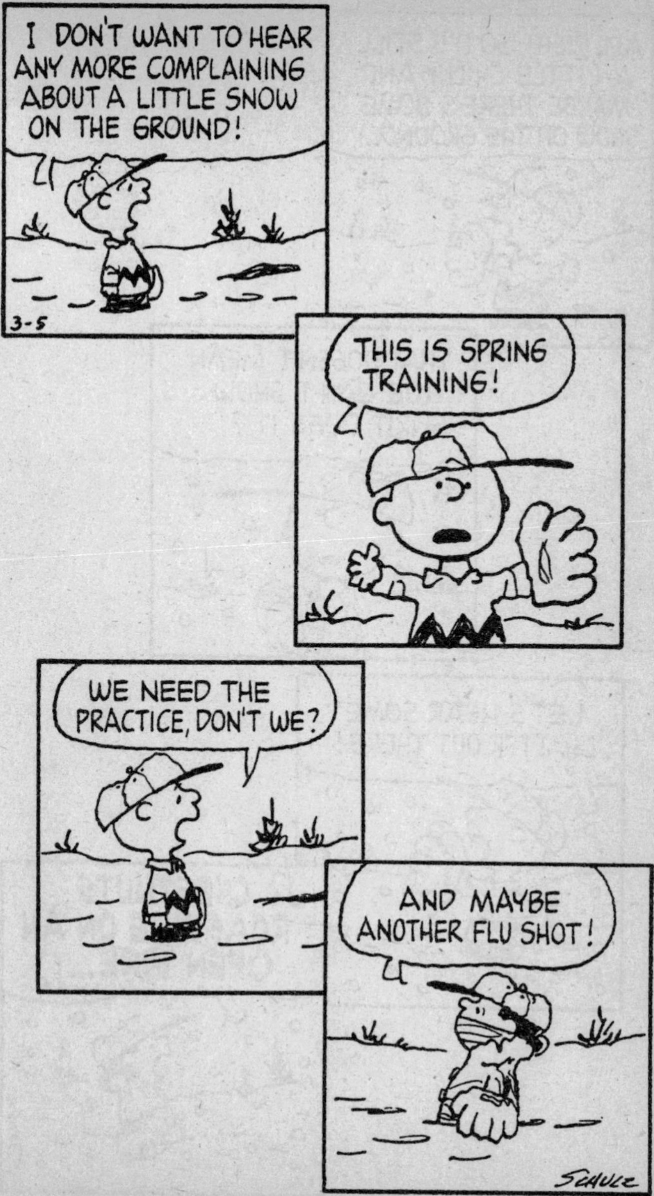
I DON'T WANT TO HEAR ANY MORE COMPLAINING ABOUT A LITTLE SNOW ON THE GROUND!
3-5
THIS IS SPRING TRAINING!
WE NEED THE PRACTICE, DON'T WE?
AND MAYBE ANOTHER FLU SHOT!
SCHULZ

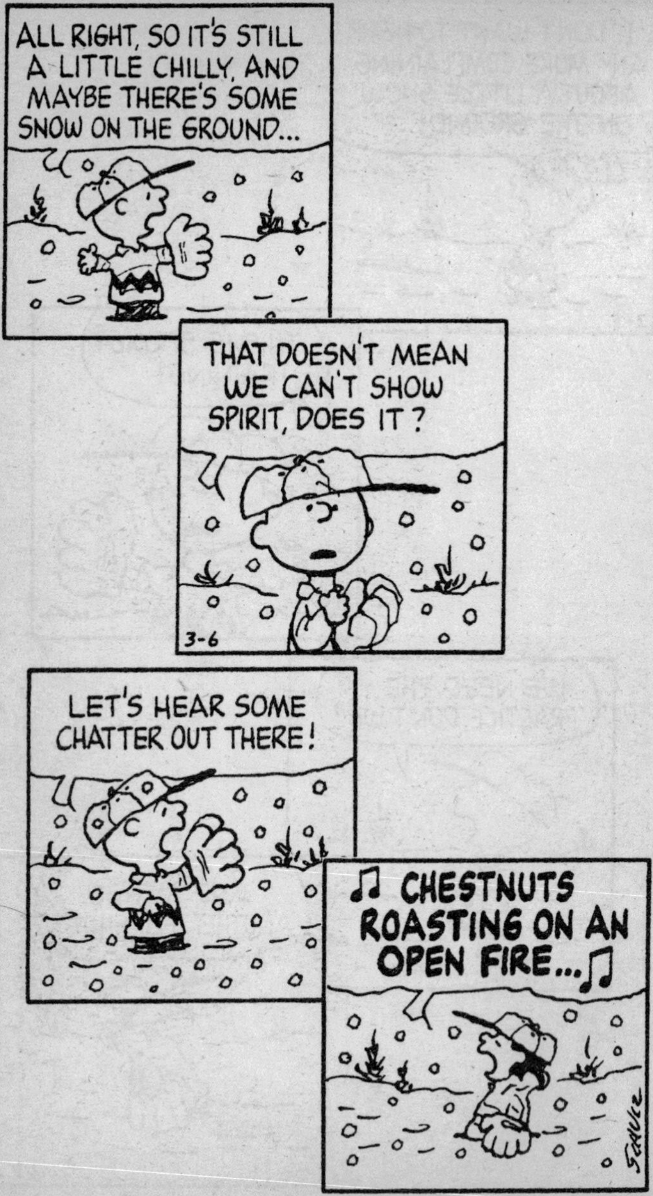
ALL RIGHT, SO IT'S STILL A LITTLE CHILLY, AND MAYBE THERE'S SOME SNOW ON THE GROUND...
THAT DOESN'T MEAN WE CAN'T SHOW SPIRIT, DOES IT?
3-6
LET'S HEAR SOME CHATTER OUT THERE!
♫ CHESTNUTS ROASTING ON AN OPEN FIRE... ♫

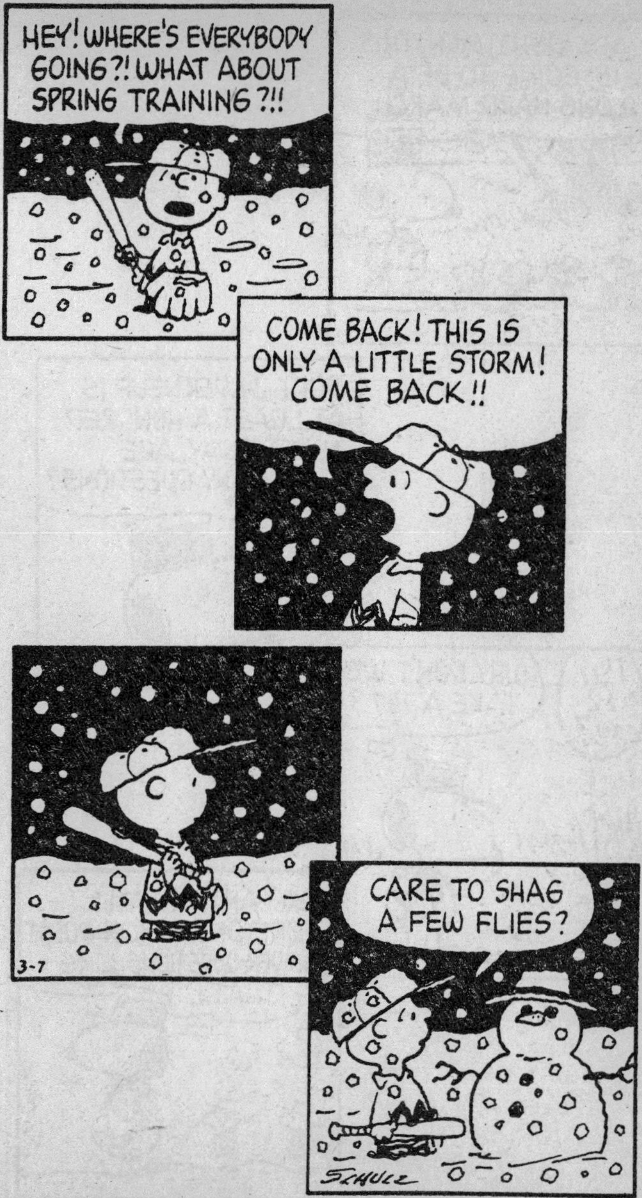
HEY! WHERE'S EVERYBODY GOING?! WHAT ABOUT SPRING TRAINING?!!
COME BACK! THIS IS ONLY A LITTLE STORM! COME BACK!!
3-7
CARE TO SHAG A FEW FLIES?
SCHULZ

ALL RIGHT, MEN, THIS IS GOING TO BE A LONG HARD MARCH..
FORT ZINDERNEUF IS AT LEAST A HUNDRED MILES AWAY..ARE THERE ANY QUESTIONS?
3-9
WHY DON'T WE TAKE A 747?
SERGEANTS IN THE FOREIGN LEGION DON'T ANSWER QUESTIONS LIKE THAT!
SCHULZ

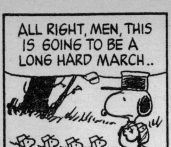

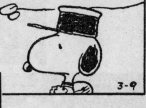

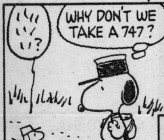

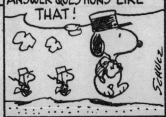

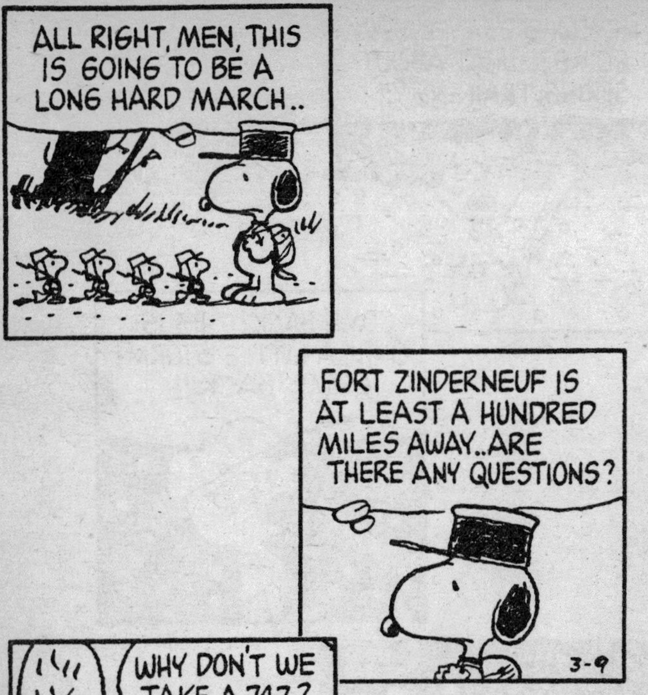

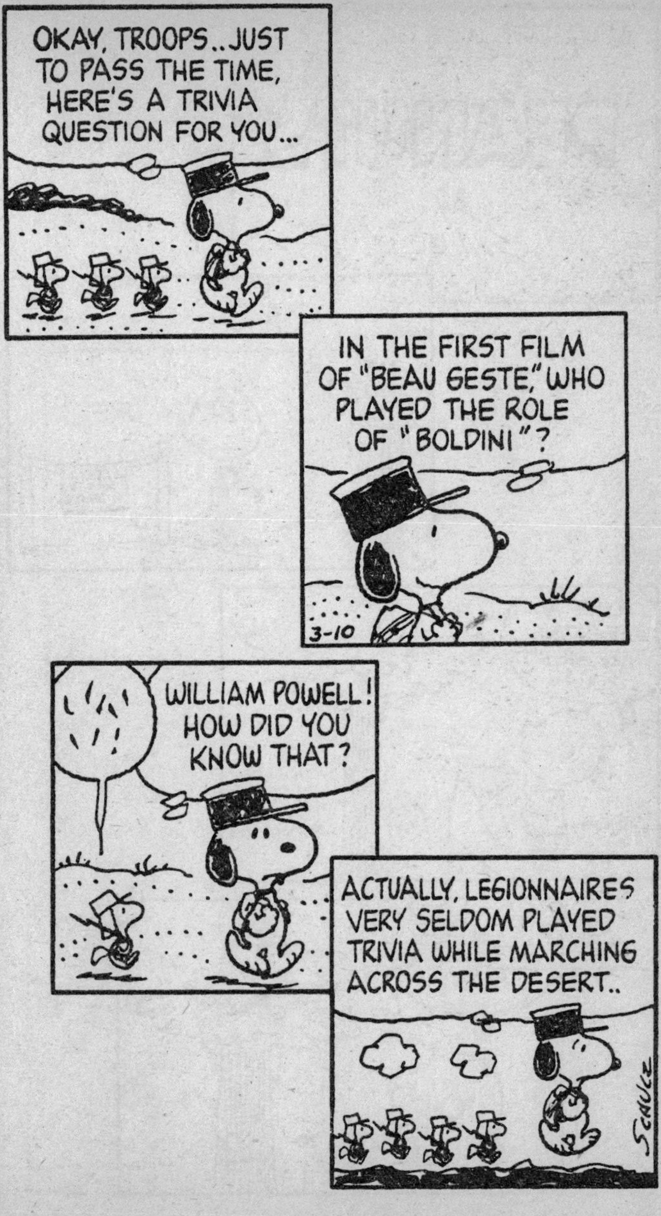
OKAY, TROOPS..JUST TO PASS THE TIME, HERE'S A TRIVIA QUESTION FOR YOU...
IN THE FIRST FILM OF "BEAU GESTE," WHO PLAYED THE ROLE OF "BOLDINI"?
3-10
WILLIAM POWELL! HOW DID YOU KNOW THAT?
ACTUALLY, LEGIONNAIRES VERY SELDOM PLAYED TRIVIA WHILE MARCHING ACROSS THE DESERT..
SCHULZ

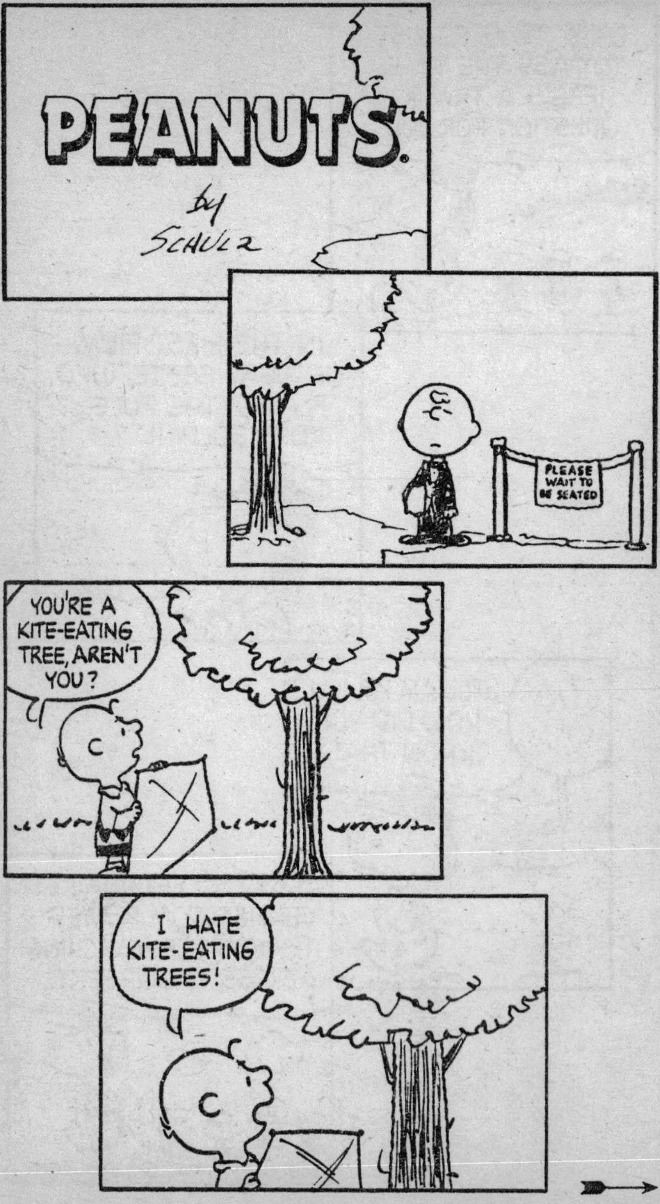
PEANUTS
by SCHULZ
PLEASE WAIT TO BE SEATED
YOU'RE A KITE-EATING TREE, AREN'T YOU?
I HATE KITE-EATING TREES!

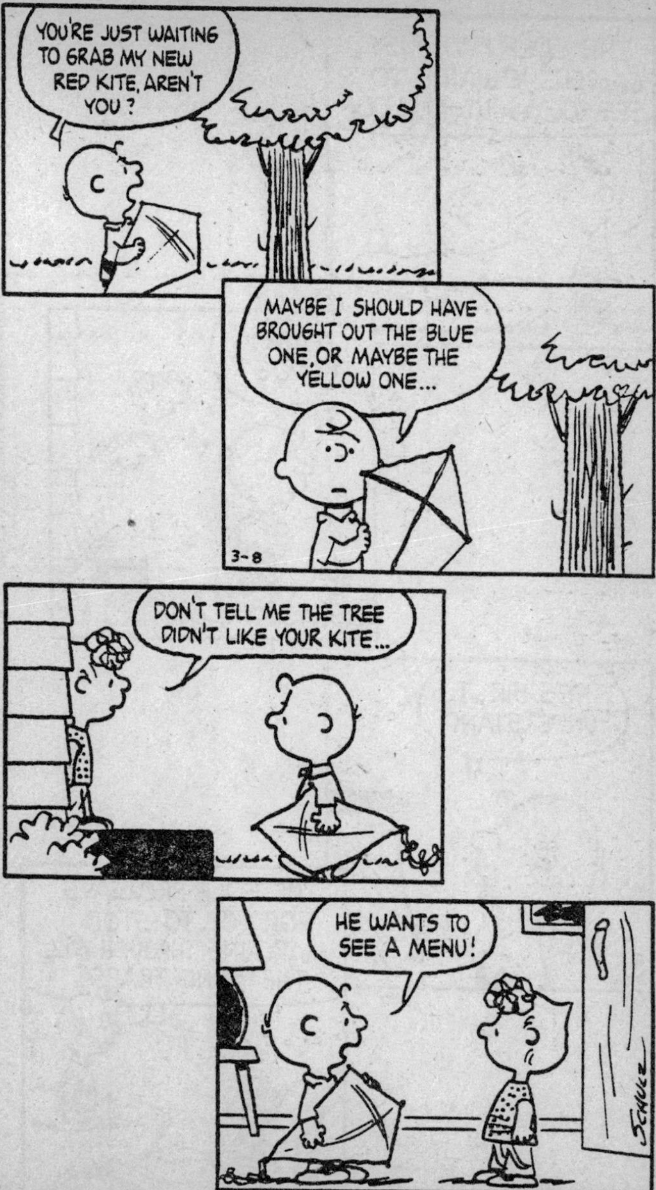
YOU'RE JUST WAITING TO GRAB MY NEW RED KITE, AREN'T YOU ?
MAYBE I SHOULD HAVE BROUGHT OUT THE BLUE ONE, OR MAYBE THE YELLOW ONE...
3-8
DON'T TELL ME THE TREE DIDN'T LIKE YOUR KITE...
HE WANTS TO SEE A MENU!
SCHULZ

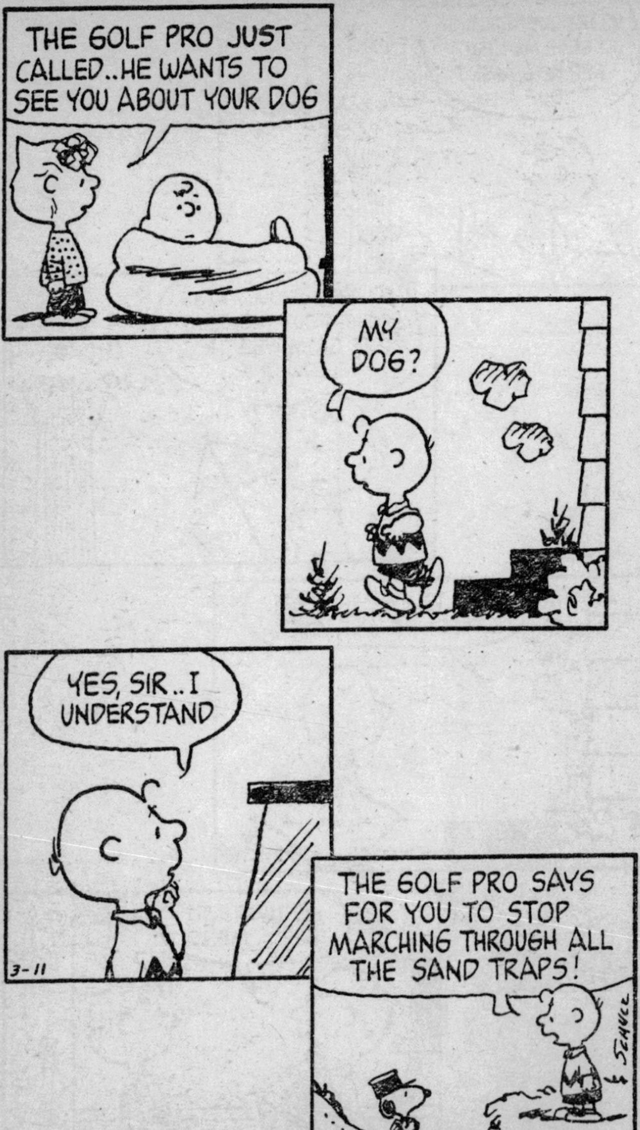
THE GOLF PRO JUST CALLED..HE WANTS TO SEE YOU ABOUT YOUR DOG
MY DOG?
YES, SIR..I UNDERSTAND
3-11
THE GOLF PRO SAYS FOR YOU TO STOP MARCHING THROUGH ALL THE SAND TRAPS!
SCHULZ

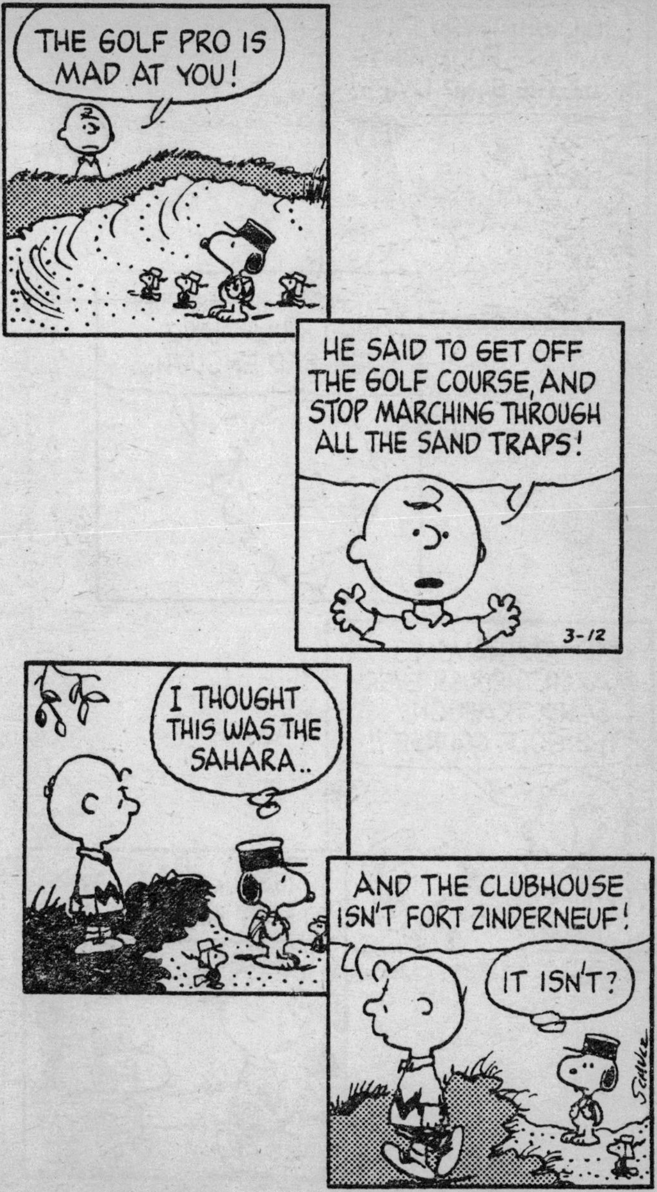
THE GOLF PRO IS MAD AT YOU!
HE SAID TO GET OFF THE GOLF COURSE, AND STOP MARCHING THROUGH ALL THE SAND TRAPS!
3-12
I THOUGHT THIS WAS THE SAHARA..
AND THE CLUBHOUSE ISN'T FORT ZINDERNEUF!
IT ISN'T?

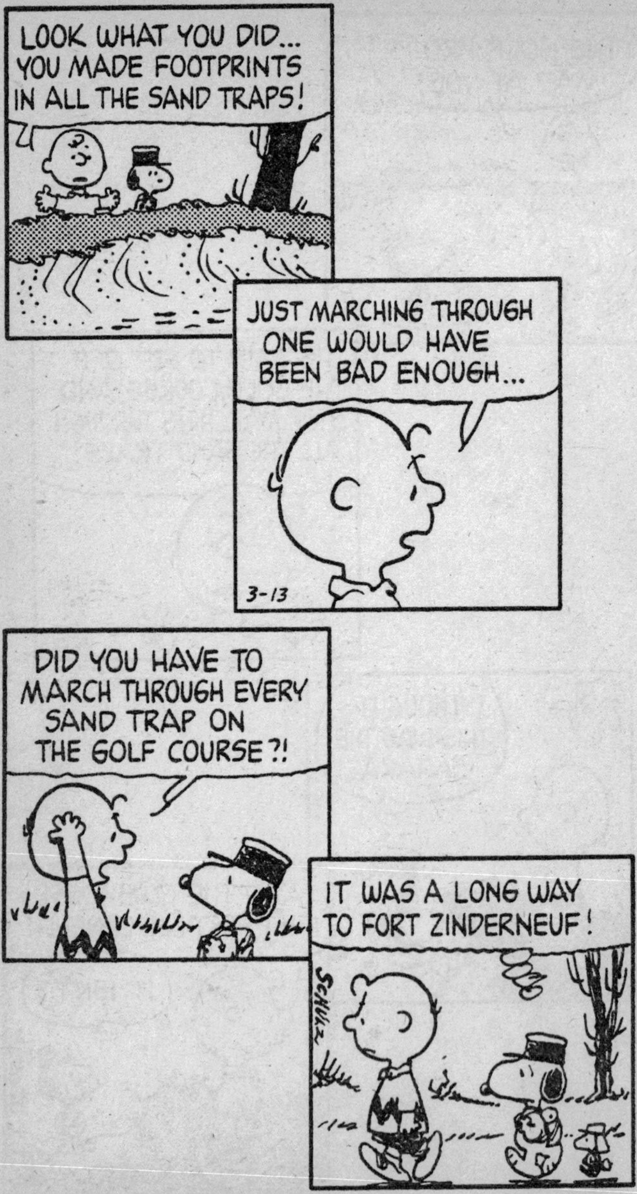
LOOK WHAT YOU DID... YOU MADE FOOTPRINTS IN ALL THE SAND TRAPS!
JUST MARCHING THROUGH ONE WOULD HAVE BEEN BAD ENOUGH...
3-13
DID YOU HAVE TO MARCH THROUGH EVERY SAND TRAP ON THE GOLF COURSE?!
IT WAS A LONG WAY TO FORT ZINDERNEUF!
SCHULZ

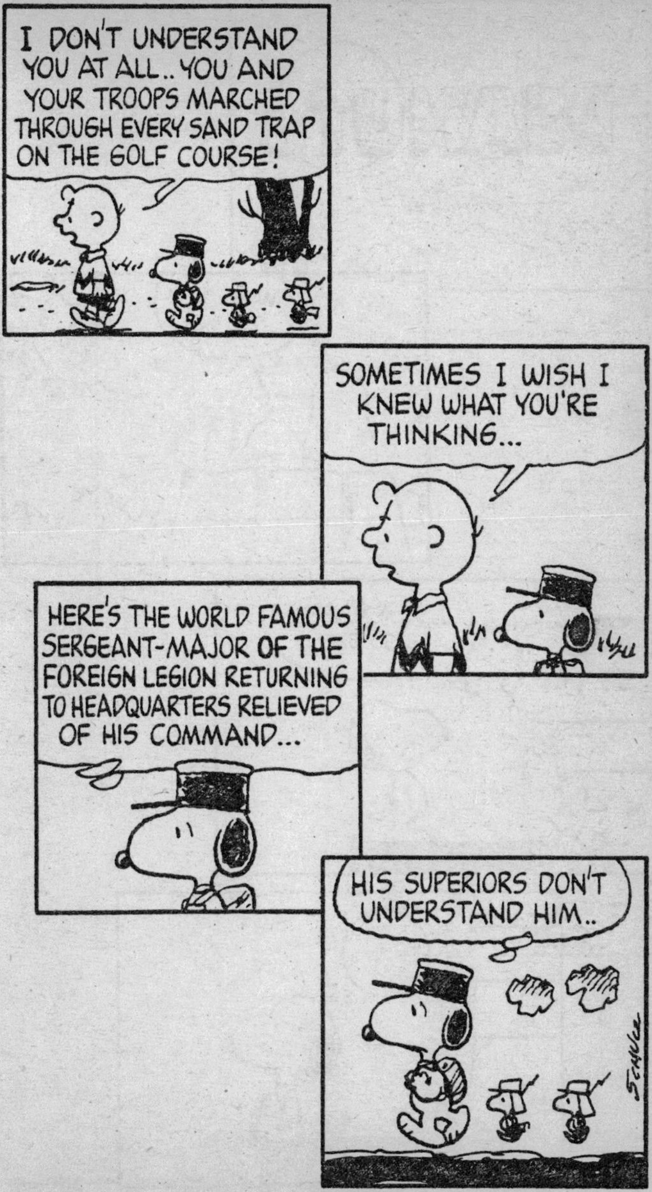
I DON'T UNDERSTAND YOU AT ALL.. YOU AND YOUR TROOPS MARCHED THROUGH EVERY SAND TRAP ON THE GOLF COURSE!
SOMETIMES I WISH I KNEW WHAT YOU'RE THINKING...
HERE'S THE WORLD FAMOUS SERGEANT-MAJOR OF THE FOREIGN LEGION RETURNING TO HEADQUARTERS RELIEVED OF HIS COMMAND...
HIS SUPERIORS DON'T UNDERSTAND HIM..

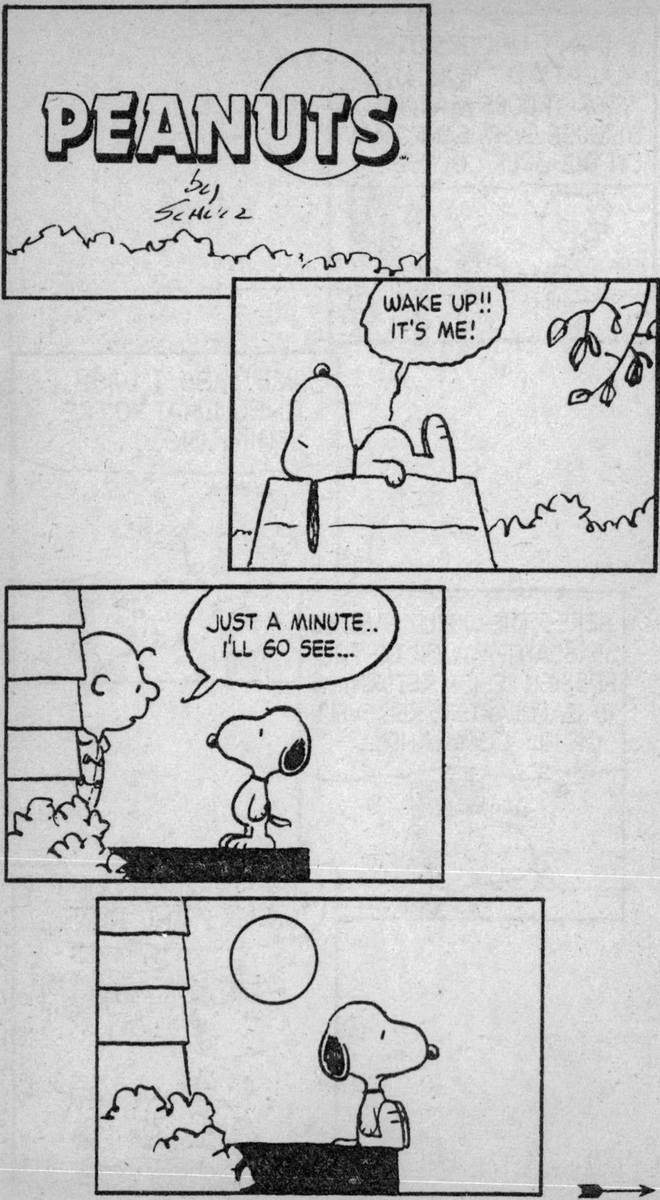
PEANUTS
by Schulz
WAKE UP!! IT'S ME!
JUST A MINUTE.. I'LL GO SEE...

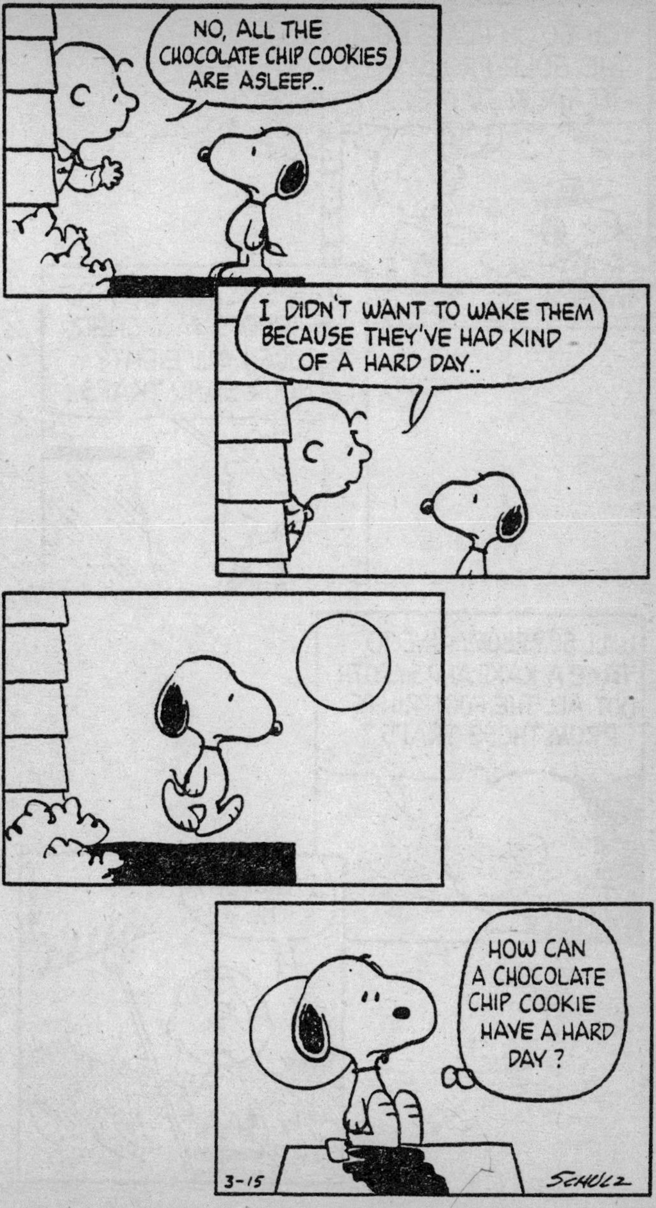
NO, ALL THE CHOCOLATE CHIP COOKIES ARE ASLEEP..
I DIDN'T WANT TO WAKE THEM BECAUSE THEY'VE HAD KIND OF A HARD DAY..
HOW CAN A CHOCOLATE CHIP COOKIE HAVE A HARD DAY?
3-15
SCHULZ

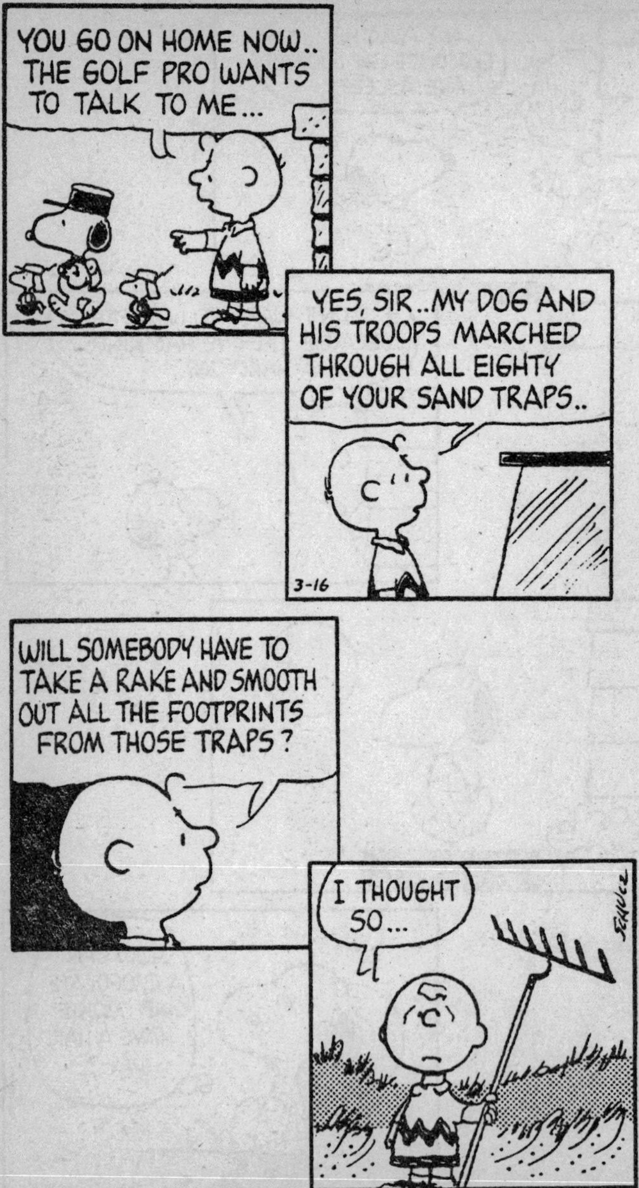

YOU GO ON HOME NOW.. THE GOLF PRO WANTS TO TALK TO ME...
YES, SIR..MY DOG AND HIS TROOPS MARCHED THROUGH ALL EIGHTY OF YOUR SAND TRAPS..
3-16
WILL SOMEBODY HAVE TO TAKE A RAKE AND SMOOTH OUT ALL THE FOOTPRINTS FROM THOSE TRAPS?
I THOUGHT SO...
SCHULZ

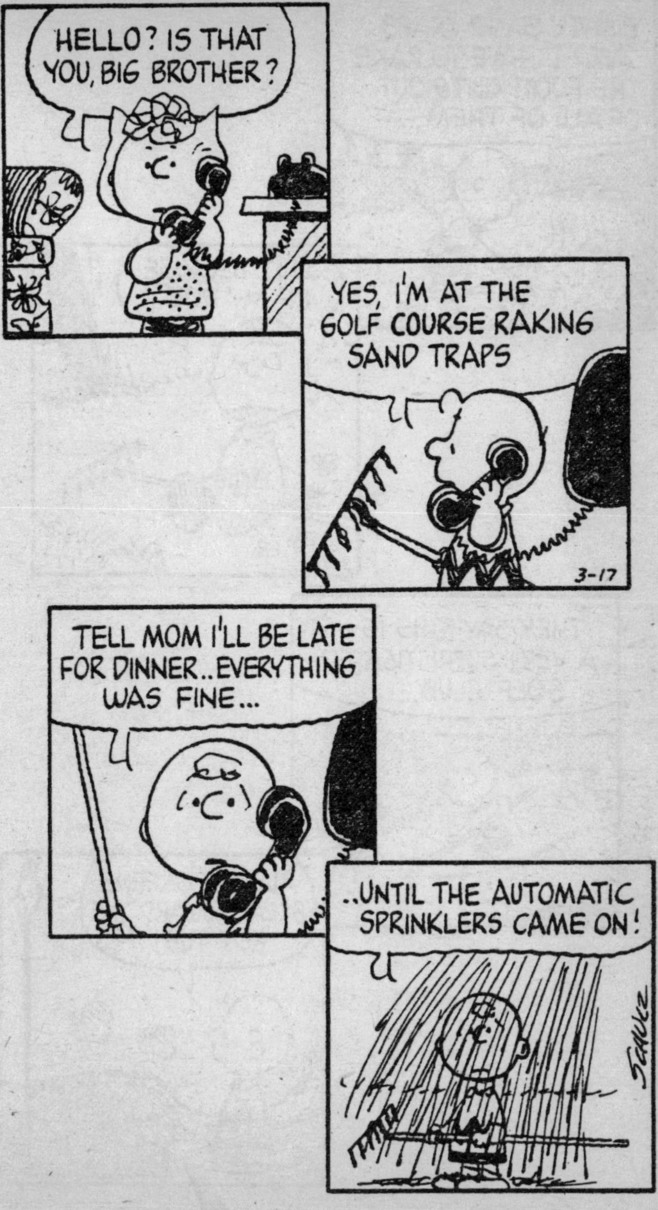

HELLO? IS THAT YOU, BIG BROTHER?
YES, I'M AT THE GOLF COURSE RAKING SAND TRAPS
3-17
TELL MOM I'LL BE LATE FOR DINNER..EVERYTHING WAS FINE...
..UNTIL THE AUTOMATIC SPRINKLERS CAME ON!
SCHULZ

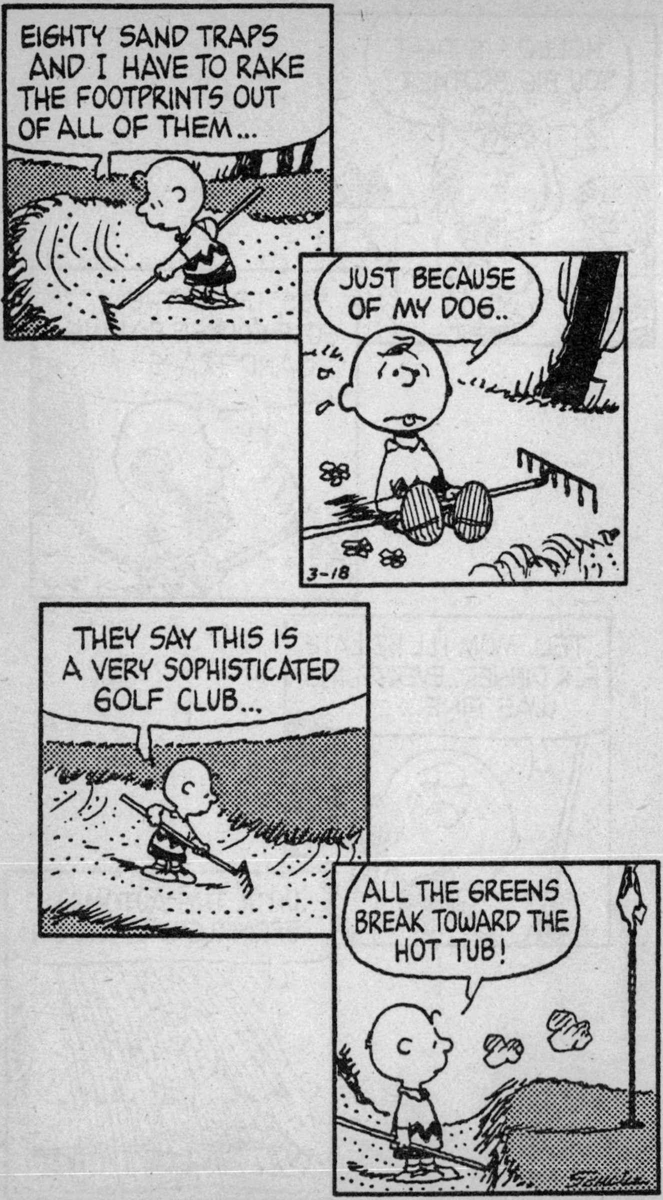
EIGHTY SAND TRAPS AND I HAVE TO RAKE THE FOOTPRINTS OUT OF ALL OF THEM...
JUST BECAUSE OF MY DOG..
3-18
THEY SAY THIS IS A VERY SOPHISTICATED GOLF CLUB...
ALL THE GREENS BREAK TOWARD THE HOT TUB!

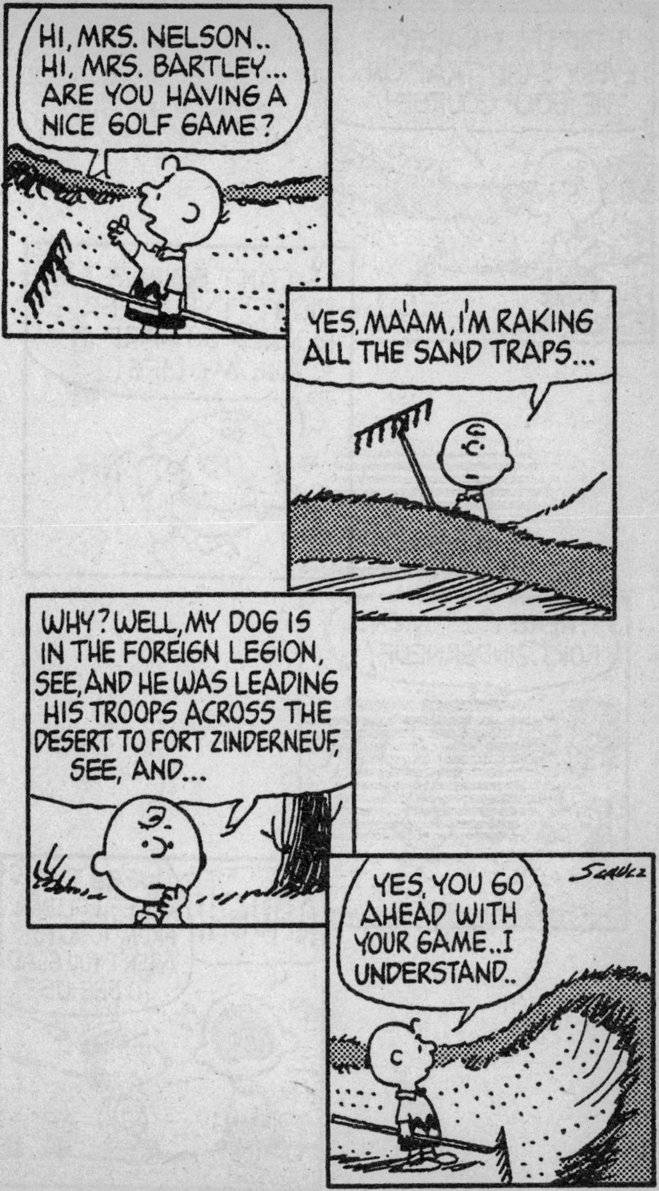
HI, MRS. NELSON.. HI, MRS. BARTLEY... ARE YOU HAVING A NICE GOLF GAME?
YES, MA'AM, I'M RAKING ALL THE SAND TRAPS...
WHY? WELL, MY DOG IS IN THE FOREIGN LEGION, SEE, AND HE WAS LEADING HIS TROOPS ACROSS THE DESERT TO FORT ZINDERNEUF, SEE, AND...
YES, YOU GO AHEAD WITH YOUR GAME..I UNDERSTAND..

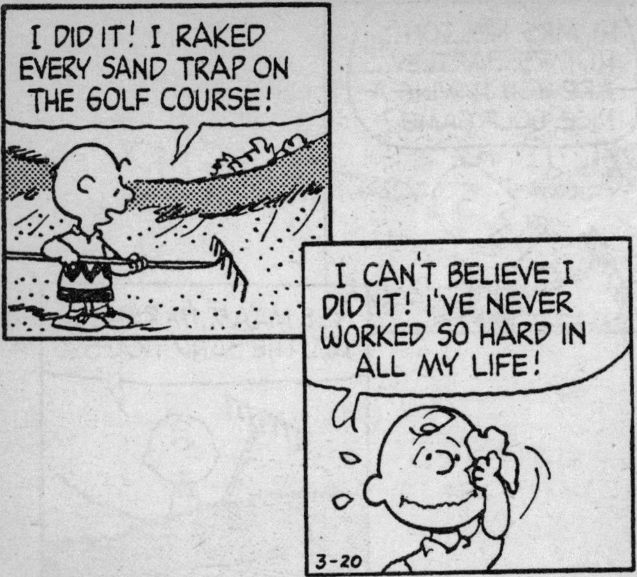
I DID IT! I RAKED EVERY SAND TRAP ON THE GOLF COURSE!
I CAN'T BELIEVE I DID IT! I'VE NEVER WORKED SO HARD IN ALL MY LIFE!
3-20

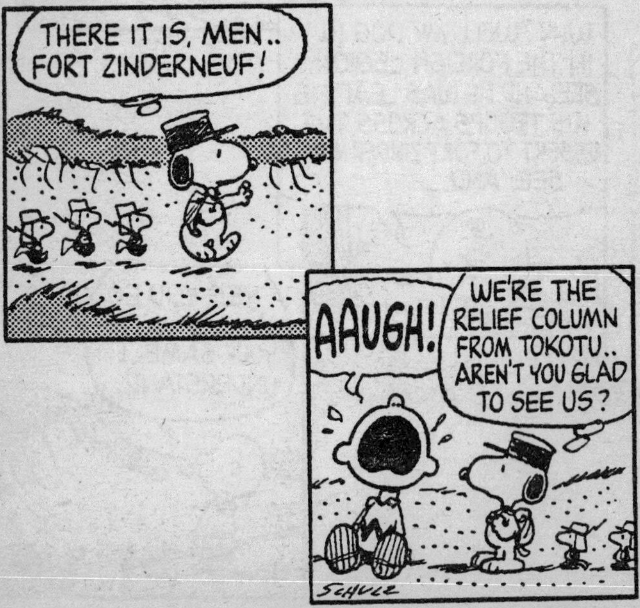
THERE IT IS, MEN.. FORT ZINDERNEUF!
AAUGH!
WE'RE THE RELIEF COLUMN FROM TOKOTU.. AREN'T YOU GLAD TO SEE US?
SCHULZ

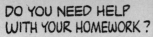
DO YOU NEED HELP WITH YOUR HOMEWORK?

I'M GOOD AT WRITING TERM PAPERS..DO YOU NEED ANY ADVICE?

GO AHEAD..ASK ME ANYTHING...

3-21

IS "GET LOST" ONE WORD OR TWO?

Schulz

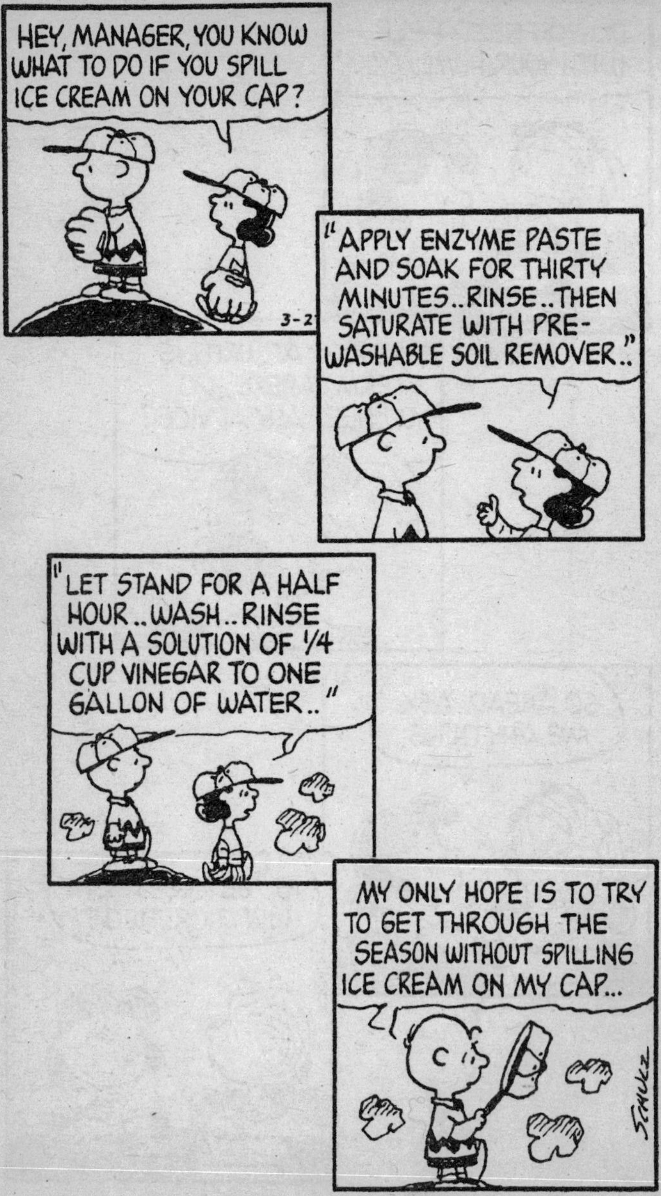
HEY, MANAGER, YOU KNOW WHAT TO DO IF YOU SPILL ICE CREAM ON YOUR CAP?
"APPLY ENZYME PASTE AND SOAK FOR THIRTY MINUTES..RINSE..THEN SATURATE WITH PRE-WASHABLE SOIL REMOVER.."
"LET STAND FOR A HALF HOUR..WASH..RINSE WITH A SOLUTION OF 1/4 CUP VINEGAR TO ONE GALLON OF WATER.."
MY ONLY HOPE IS TO TRY TO GET THROUGH THE SEASON WITHOUT SPILLING ICE CREAM ON MY CAP...

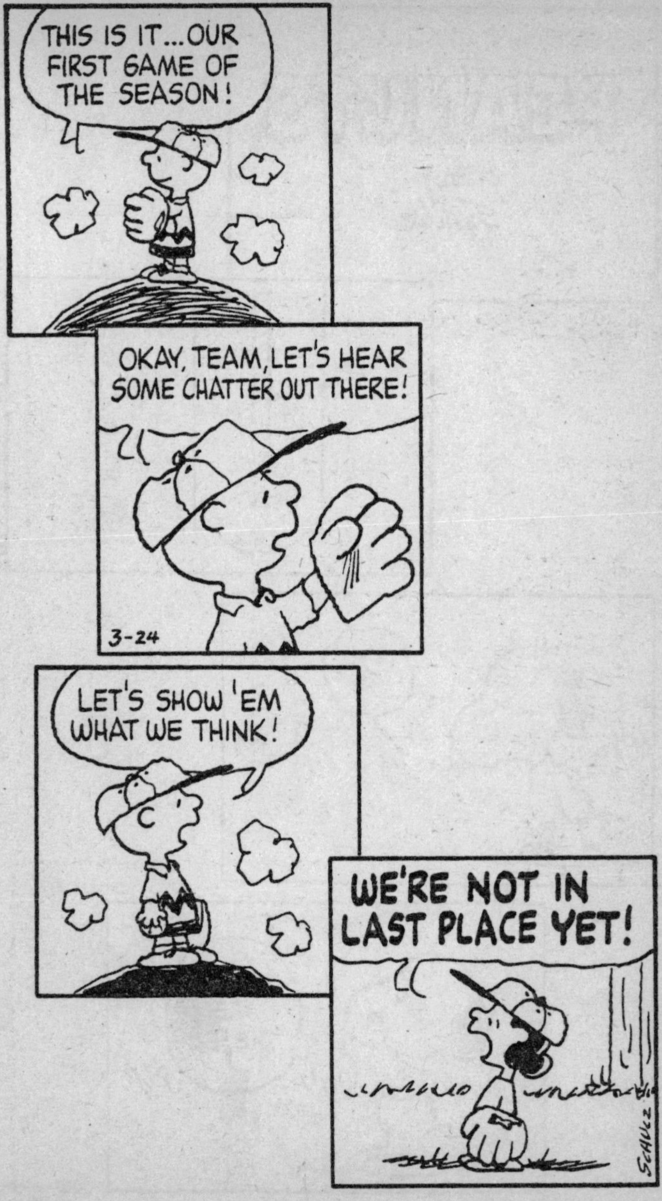
THIS IS IT...OUR FIRST GAME OF THE SEASON!
OKAY, TEAM, LET'S HEAR SOME CHATTER OUT THERE!
3-24
LET'S SHOW 'EM WHAT WE THINK!
WE'RE NOT IN LAST PLACE YET!
SCHULZ

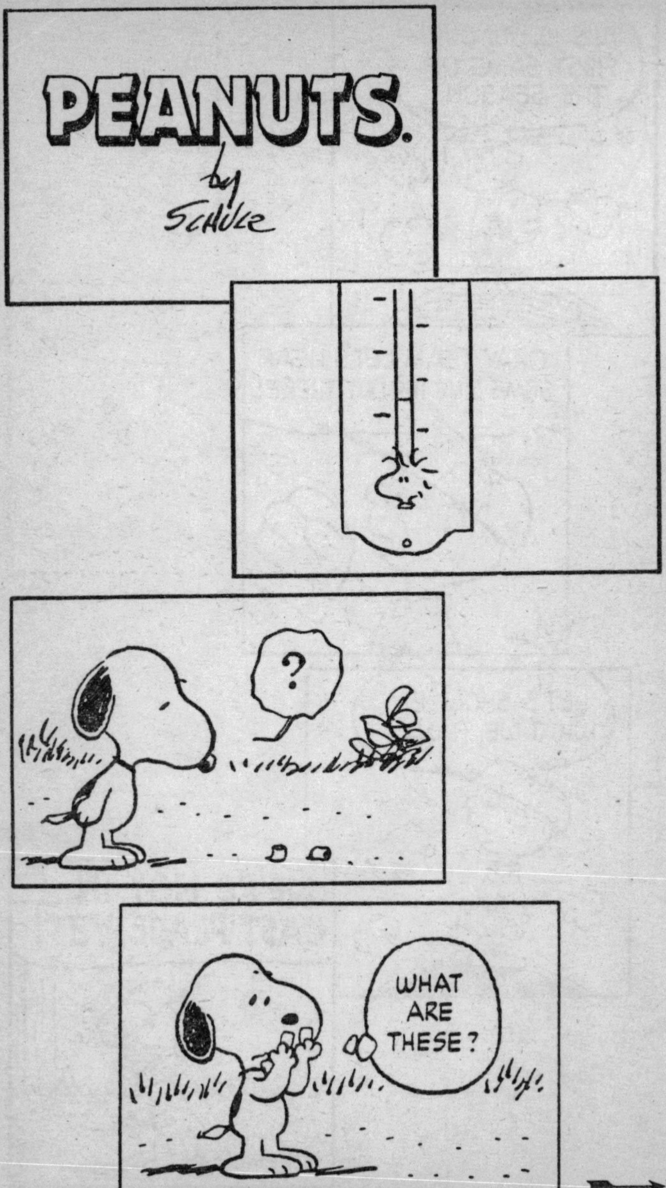
PEANUTS.
by Schulz
?
WHAT ARE THESE?

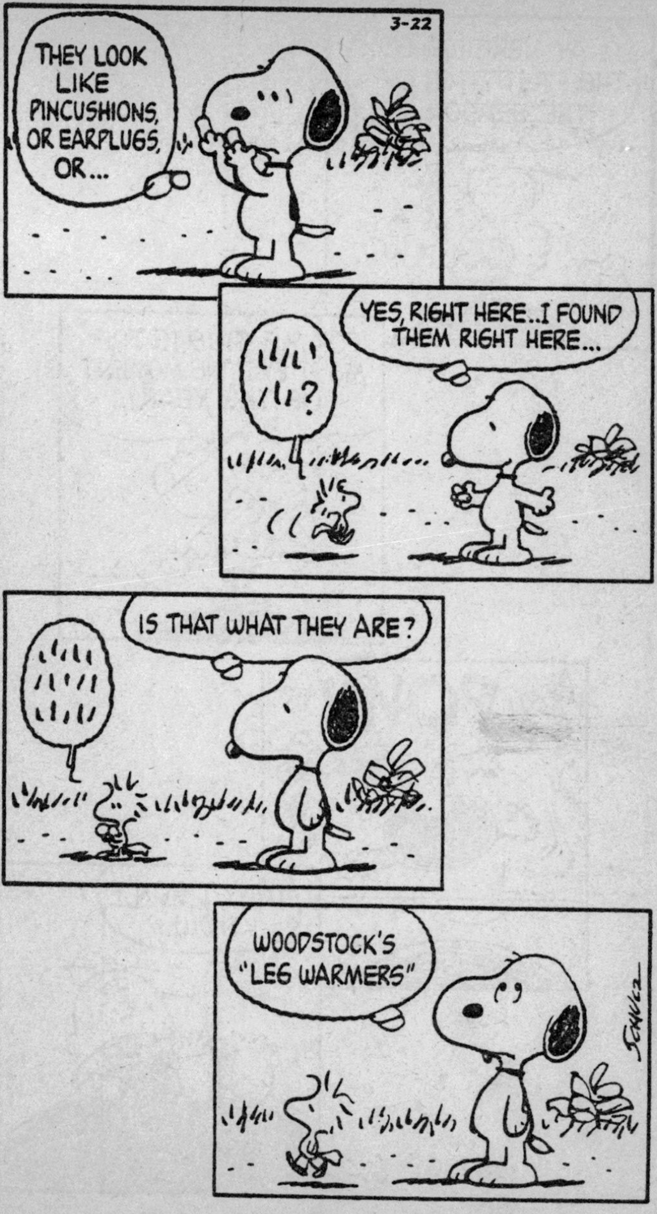
3-22
THEY LOOK LIKE PINCUSHIONS, OR EARPLUGS, OR...
YES, RIGHT HERE..I FOUND THEM RIGHT HERE...
IS THAT WHAT THEY ARE?
WOODSTOCK'S "LEG WARMERS"
SCHULZ

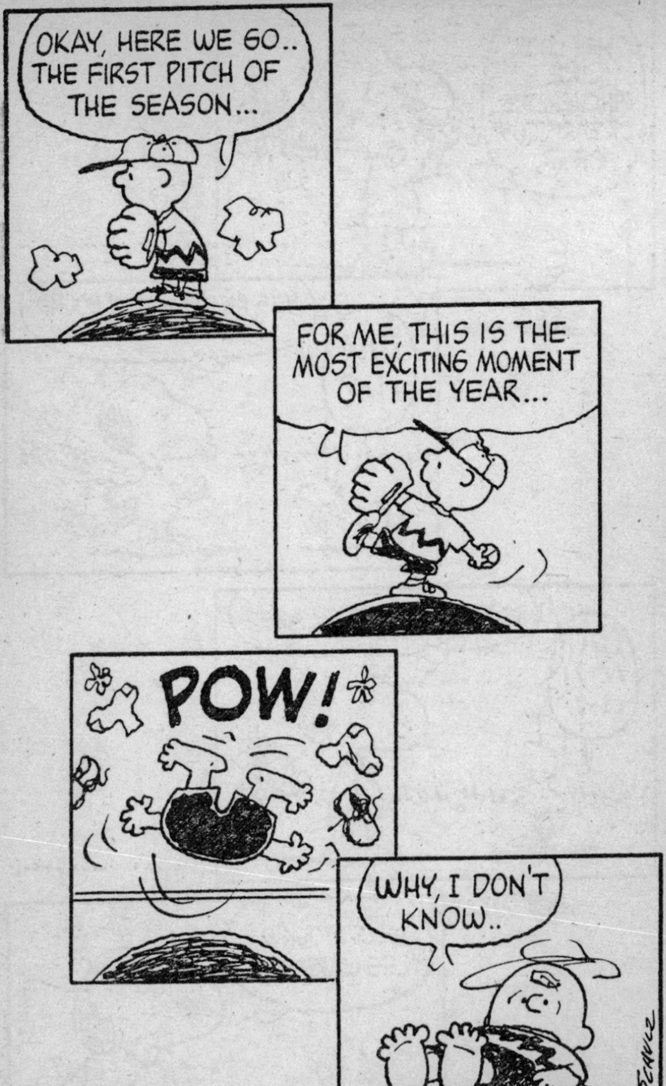
OKAY, HERE WE GO.. THE FIRST PITCH OF THE SEASON...
FOR ME, THIS IS THE MOST EXCITING MOMENT OF THE YEAR...
POW!
WHY, I DON'T KNOW..
SCHULZ

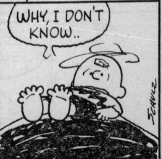

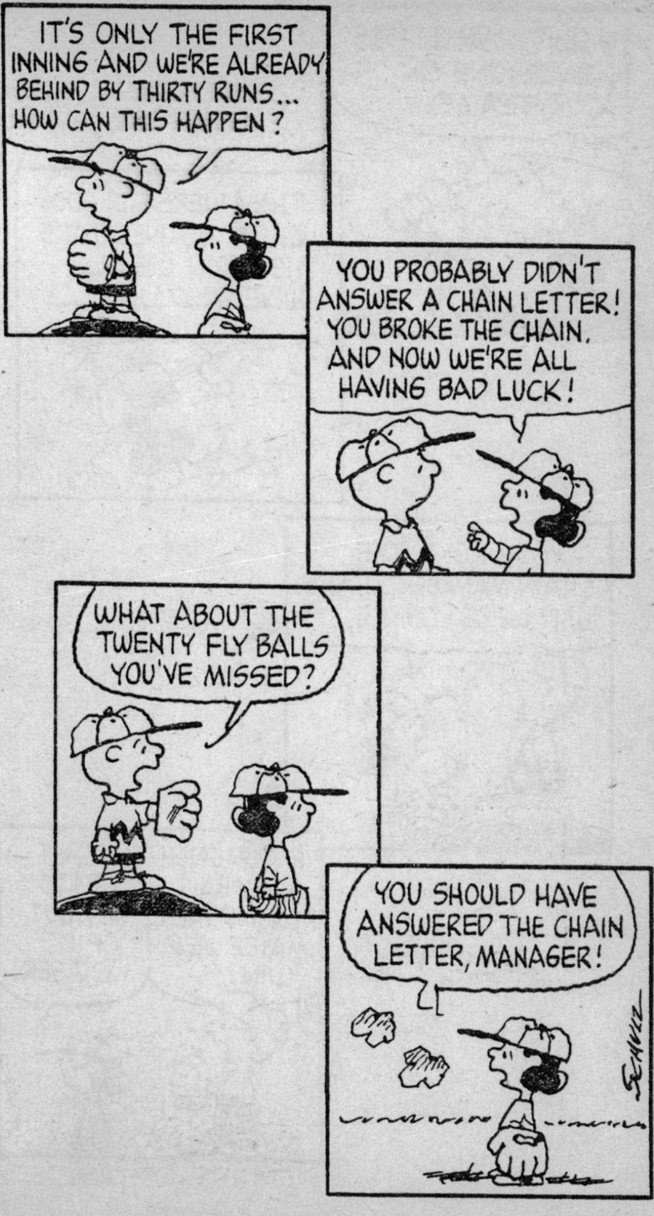
IT'S ONLY THE FIRST INNING AND WE'RE ALREADY BEHIND BY THIRTY RUNS... HOW CAN THIS HAPPEN?
YOU PROBABLY DIDN'T ANSWER A CHAIN LETTER! YOU BROKE THE CHAIN, AND NOW WE'RE ALL HAVING BAD LUCK!
WHAT ABOUT THE TWENTY FLY BALLS YOU'VE MISSED?
YOU SHOULD HAVE ANSWERED THE CHAIN LETTER, MANAGER!
SCHULZ

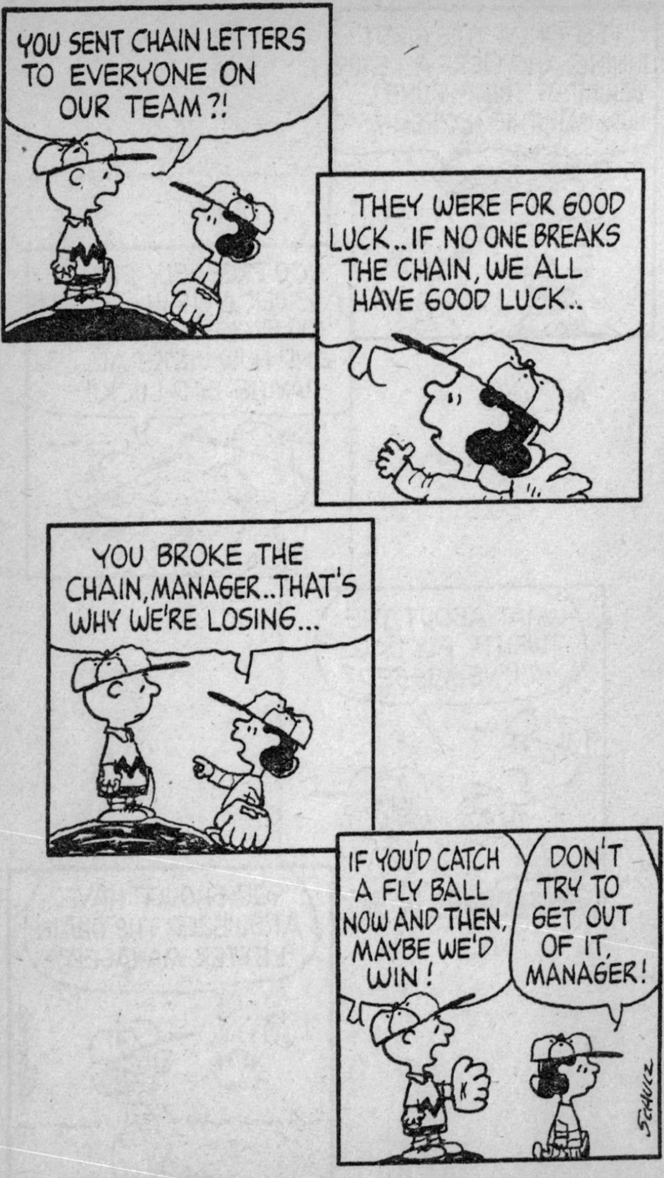
YOU SENT CHAIN LETTERS TO EVERYONE ON OUR TEAM?!
THEY WERE FOR GOOD LUCK..IF NO ONE BREAKS THE CHAIN, WE ALL HAVE GOOD LUCK..
YOU BROKE THE CHAIN, MANAGER..THAT'S WHY WE'RE LOSING...
IF YOU'D CATCH A FLY BALL NOW AND THEN, MAYBE WE'D WIN!
DON'T TRY TO GET OUT OF IT, MANAGER!
SCHULZ

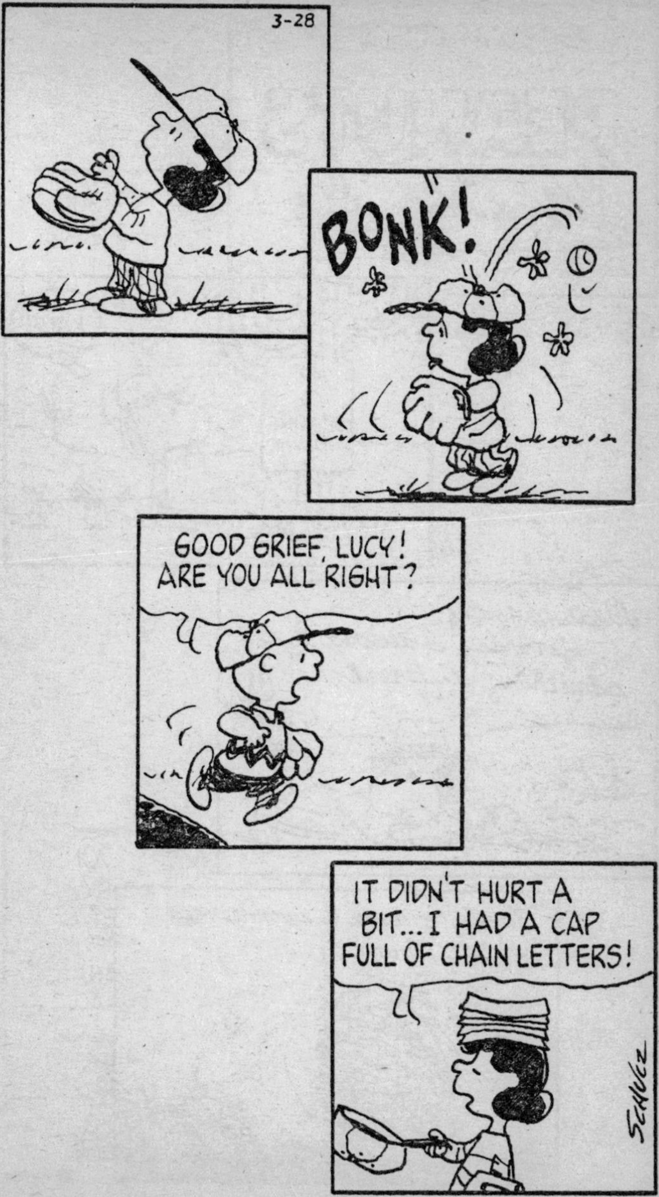
3-28
BONK!
GOOD GRIEF, LUCY! ARE YOU ALL RIGHT?
IT DIDN'T HURT A BIT... I HAD A CAP FULL OF CHAIN LETTERS!
SCHULZ

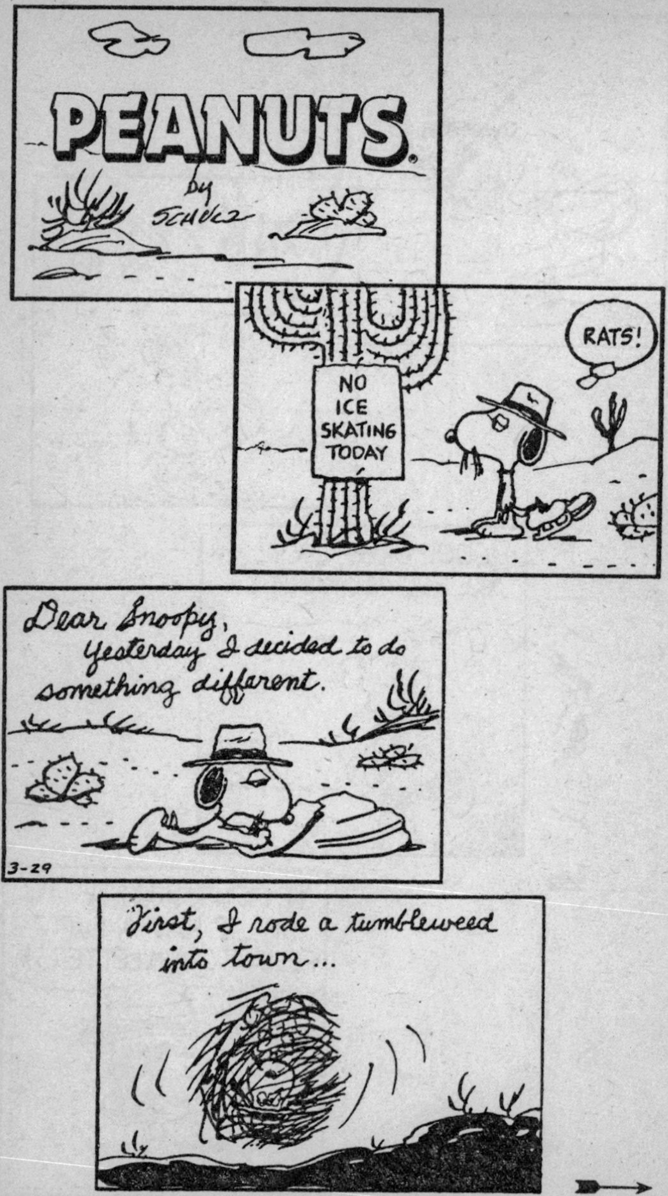
PEANUTS
by SCHULZ
NO ICE SKATING TODAY
RATS!
Dear Snoopy,
Yesterday I decided to do something differant.
3-29
First, I rode a tumbleweed into town...

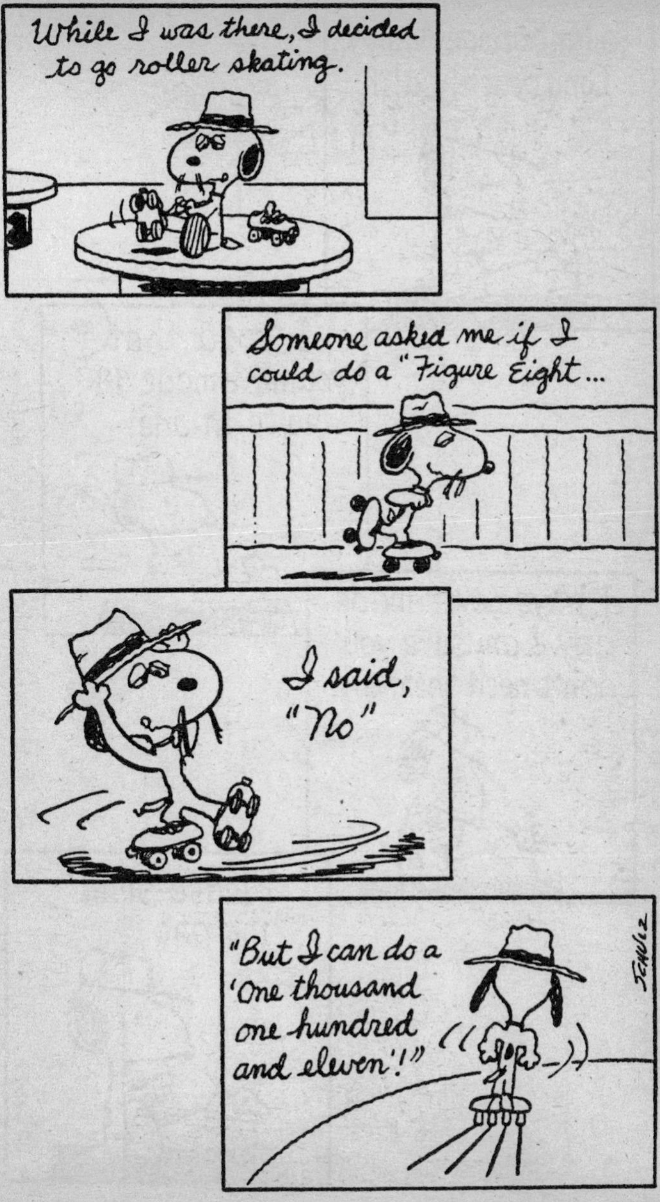
While I was there, I decided to go roller skating.
Someone asked me if I could do a "Figure Eight...
I said, "No"
"But I can do a 'One thousand one hundred and eleven'!"
SCHULZ

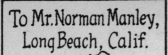

To Mr. Norman Manley, Long Beach, Calif.

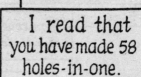

I read that you have made 58 holes-in-one.

I have never made any. I am sure you don't need them all.

Please send me one.

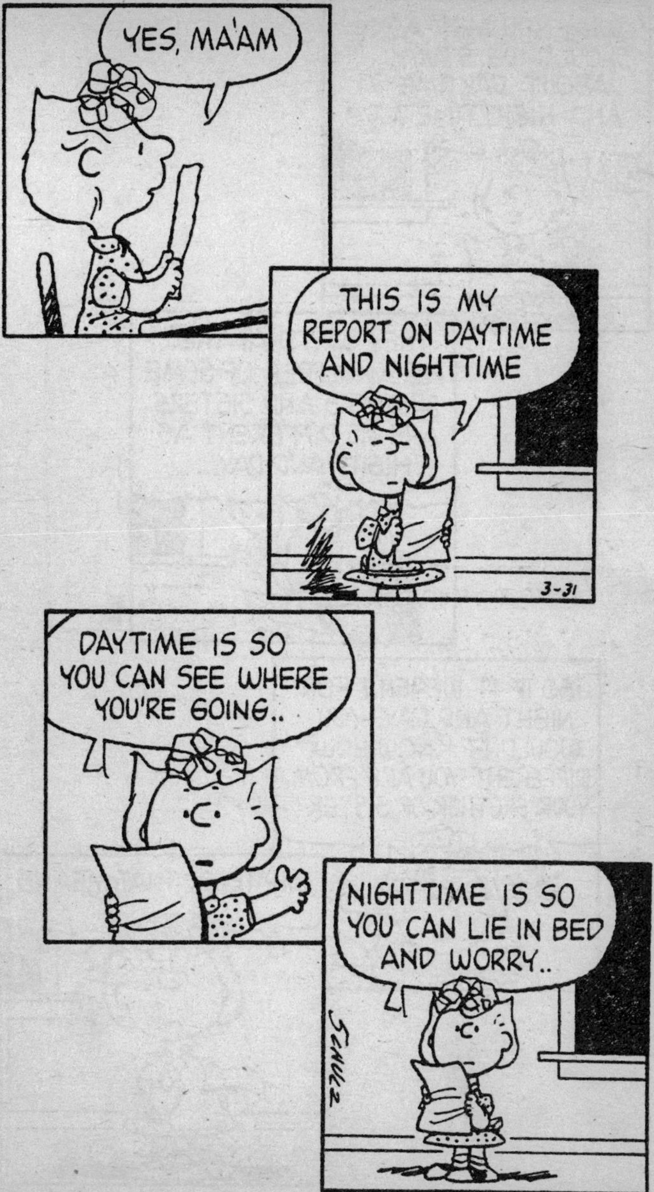
YES, MA'AM
THIS IS MY REPORT ON DAYTIME AND NIGHTTIME
3-31
DAYTIME IS SO YOU CAN SEE WHERE YOU'RE GOING..
NIGHTTIME IS SO YOU CAN LIE IN BED AND WORRY..
SCHULZ

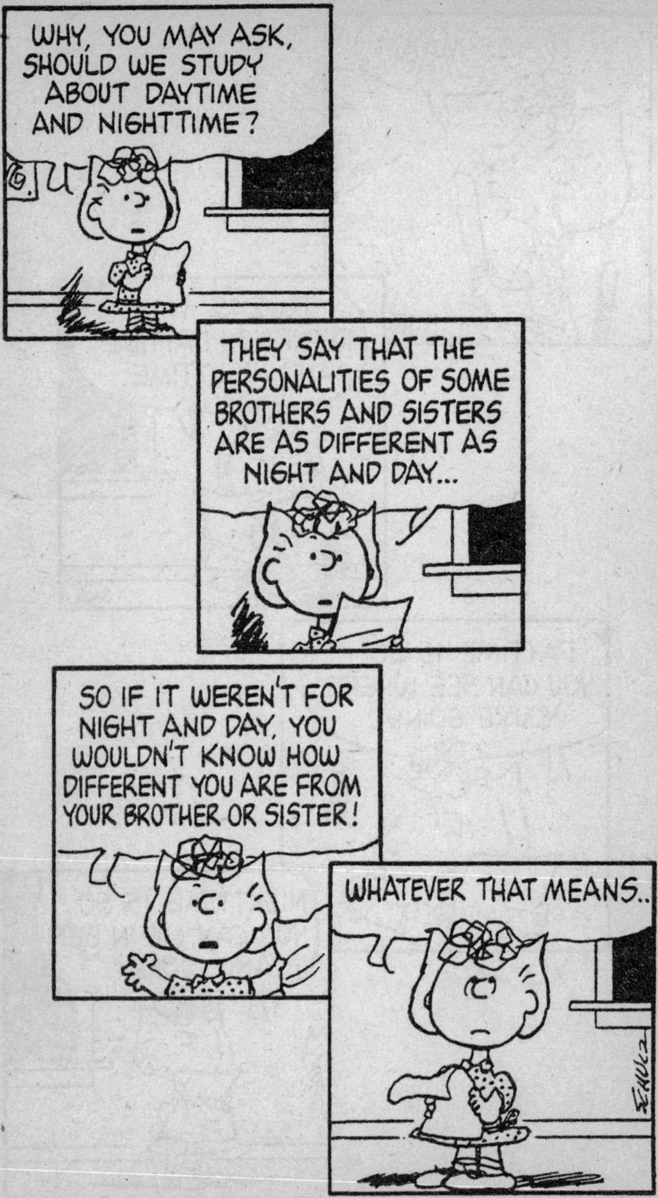
WHY, YOU MAY ASK, SHOULD WE STUDY ABOUT DAYTIME AND NIGHTTIME?
THEY SAY THAT THE PERSONALITIES OF SOME BROTHERS AND SISTERS ARE AS DIFFERENT AS NIGHT AND DAY...
SO IF IT WEREN'T FOR NIGHT AND DAY, YOU WOULDN'T KNOW HOW DIFFERENT YOU ARE FROM YOUR BROTHER OR SISTER!
WHATEVER THAT MEANS..

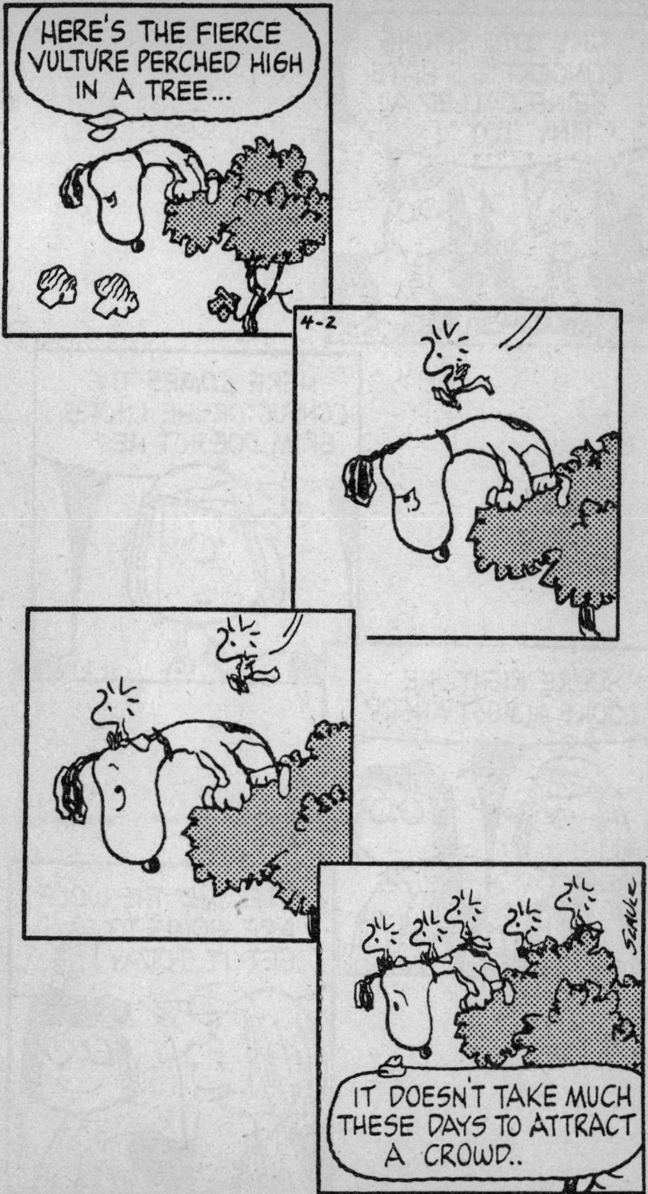
HERE'S THE FIERCE VULTURE PERCHED HIGH IN A TREE...
4-2
IT DOESN'T TAKE MUCH THESE DAYS TO ATTRACT A CROWD..
SCHULZ

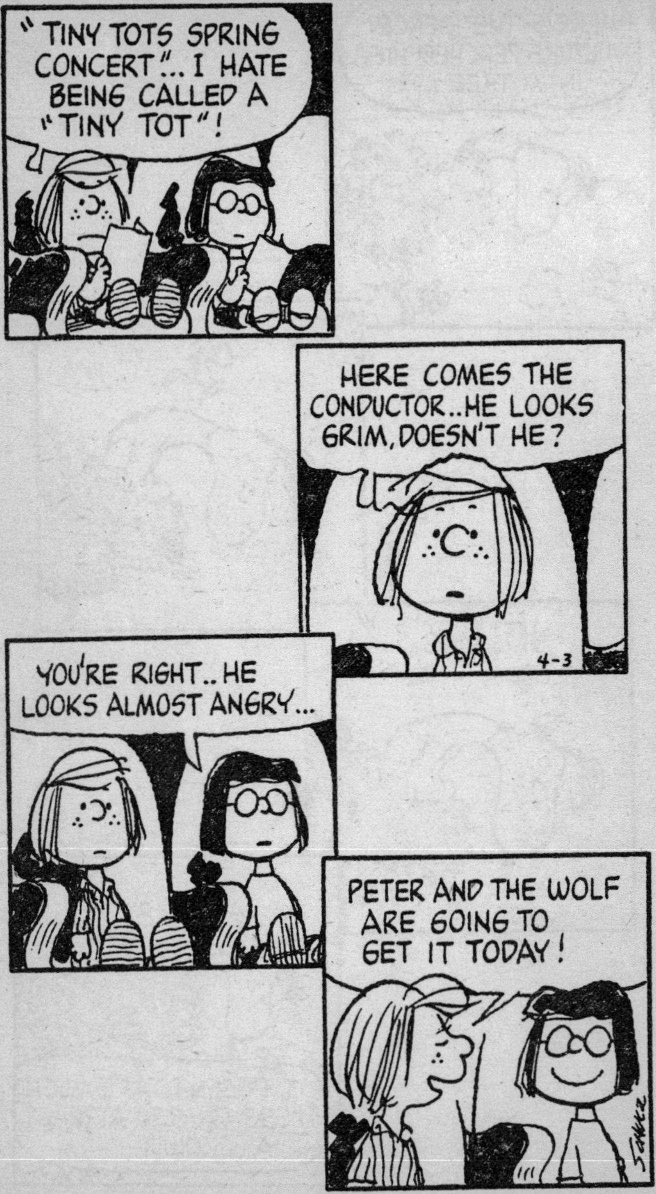
"TINY TOTS SPRING CONCERT"... I HATE BEING CALLED A "TINY TOT"!
HERE COMES THE CONDUCTOR..HE LOOKS GRIM, DOESN'T HE?
4-3
YOU'RE RIGHT.. HE LOOKS ALMOST ANGRY...
PETER AND THE WOLF ARE GOING TO GET IT TODAY!
SCHULZ

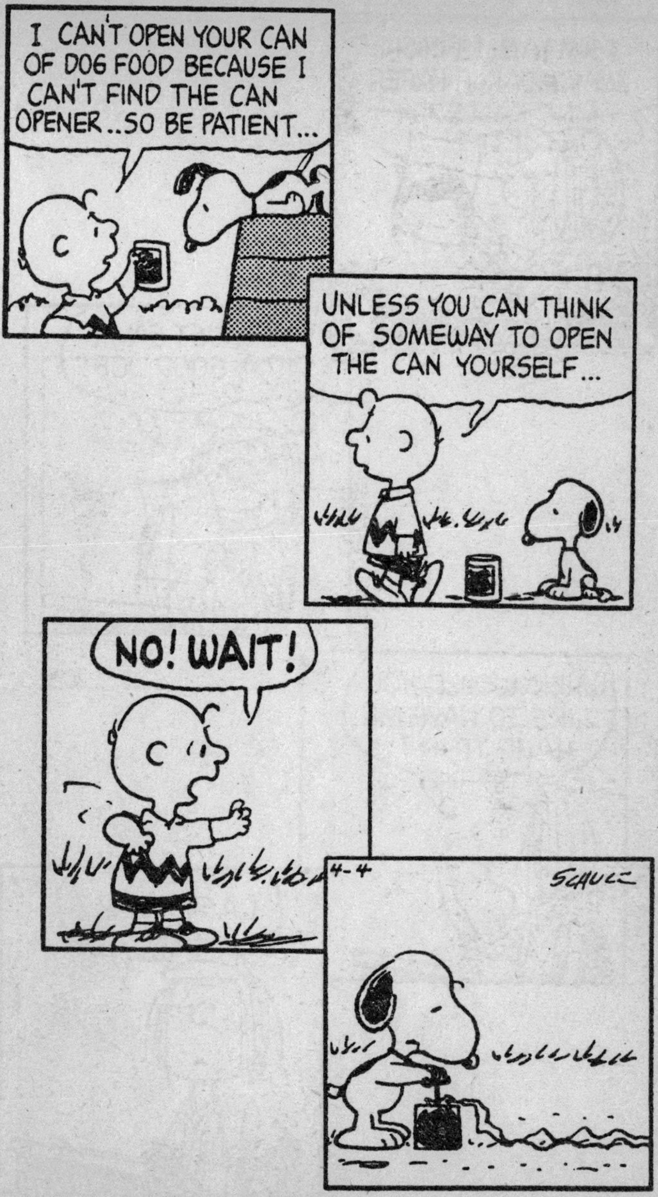
I CAN'T OPEN YOUR CAN OF DOG FOOD BECAUSE I CAN'T FIND THE CAN OPENER...SO BE PATIENT...
UNLESS YOU CAN THINK OF SOMEWAY TO OPEN THE CAN YOURSELF...
NO! WAIT!
4-4
SCHULZ

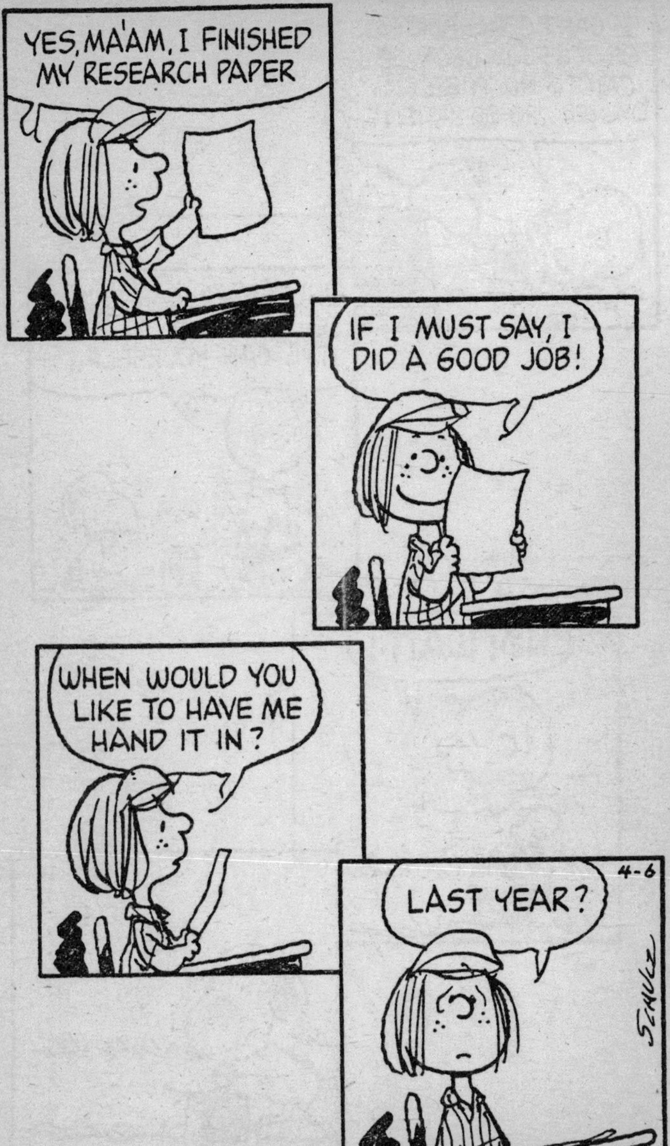
YES, MA'AM, I FINISHED MY RESEARCH PAPER
IF I MUST SAY, I DID A GOOD JOB!
WHEN WOULD YOU LIKE TO HAVE ME HAND IT IN?
4-6
LAST YEAR?
SCHULZ

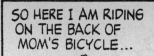

SO HERE I AM RIDING ON THE BACK OF MOM'S BICYCLE...

NOW IT'S A SHOPPING CART IN THE SUPERMARKET...

NOW IT'S A STROLLER THROUGH THE MALL..THEN, BACK ON THE BICYCLE...

SOMETIMES I GO A WHOLE DAY WITHOUT EVER TOUCHING THE GROUND!

4-7

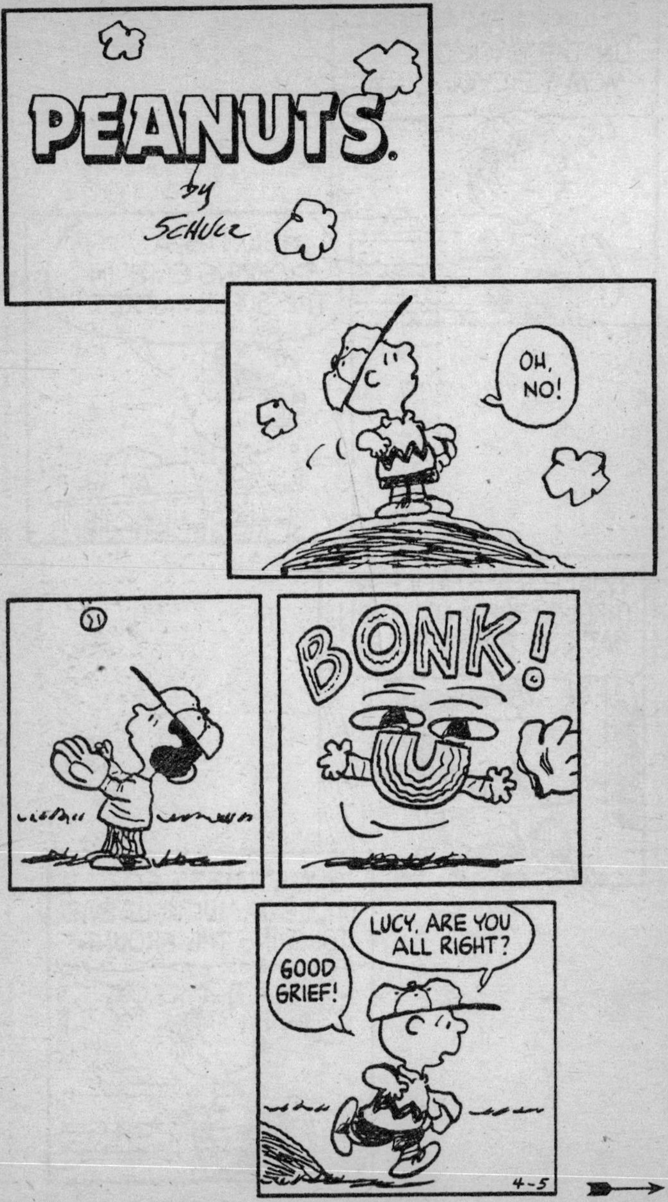
PEANUTS
by SCHULZ
OH, NO!
BONK!
GOOD GRIEF!
LUCY, ARE YOU ALL RIGHT?
4-5

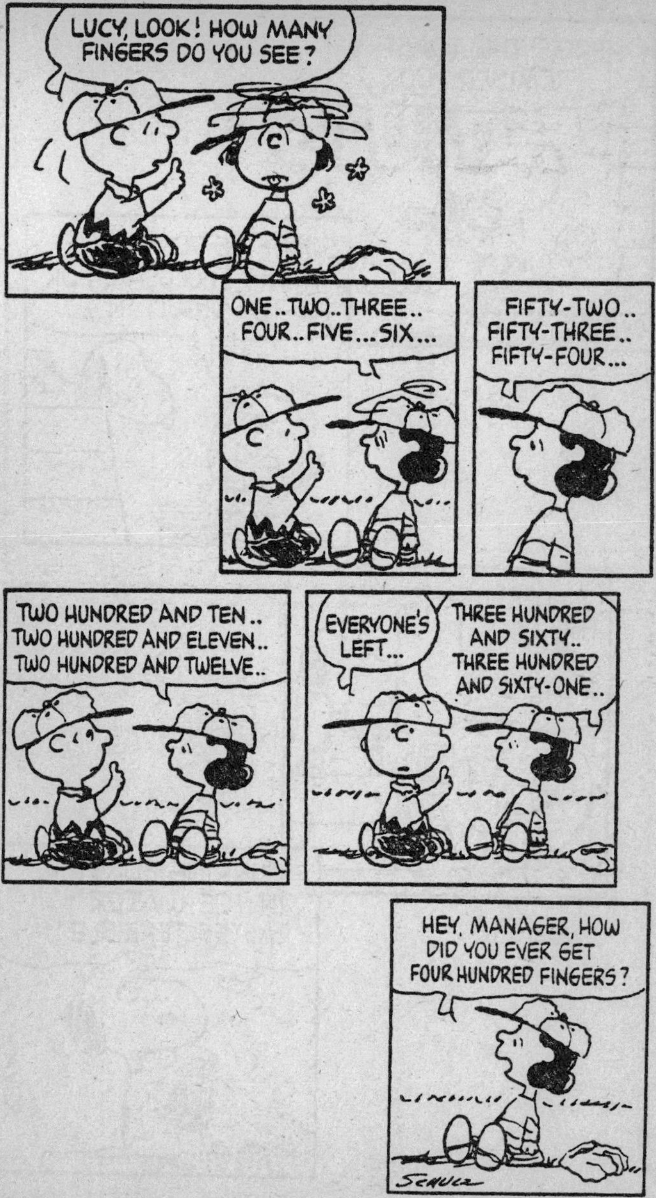
LUCY, LOOK! HOW MANY FINGERS DO YOU SEE?
ONE..TWO..THREE.. FOUR..FIVE....SIX....
FIFTY-TWO.. FIFTY-THREE.. FIFTY-FOUR...
TWO HUNDRED AND TEN.. TWO HUNDRED AND ELEVEN.. TWO HUNDRED AND TWELVE..
EVERYONE'S LEFT...
THREE HUNDRED AND SIXTY.. THREE HUNDRED AND SIXTY-ONE..
HEY, MANAGER, HOW DID YOU EVER GET FOUR HUNDRED FINGERS?
SCHULZ

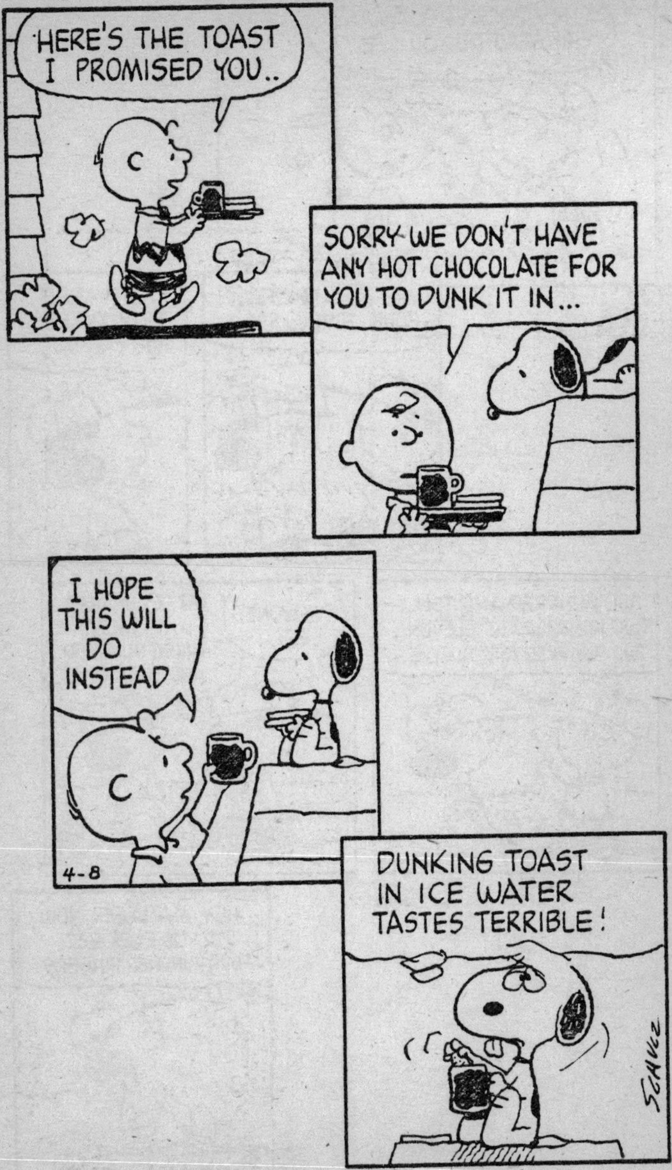
HERE'S THE TOAST I PROMISED YOU..
SORRY WE DON'T HAVE ANY HOT CHOCOLATE FOR YOU TO DUNK IT IN...
I HOPE THIS WILL DO INSTEAD
4-8
DUNKING TOAST IN ICE WATER TASTES TERRIBLE!
SCHULZ

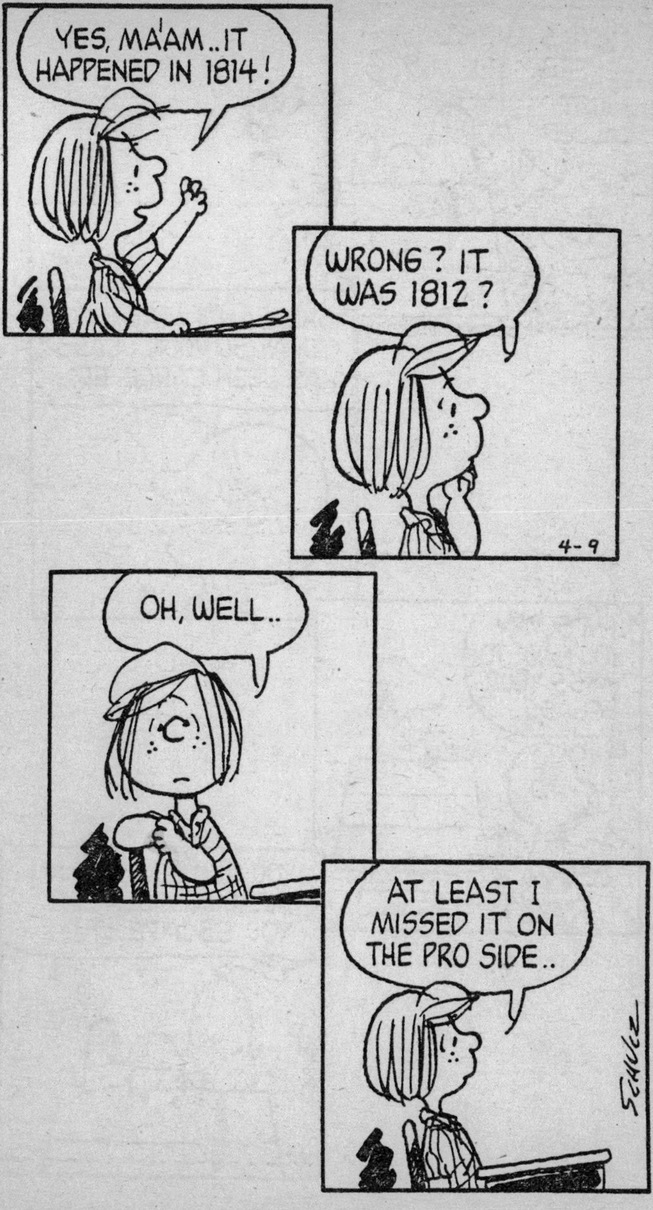
YES, MA'AM..IT HAPPENED IN 1814!
WRONG? IT WAS 1812?
4-9
OH, WELL..
AT LEAST I MISSED IT ON THE PRO SIDE..
SCHULZ

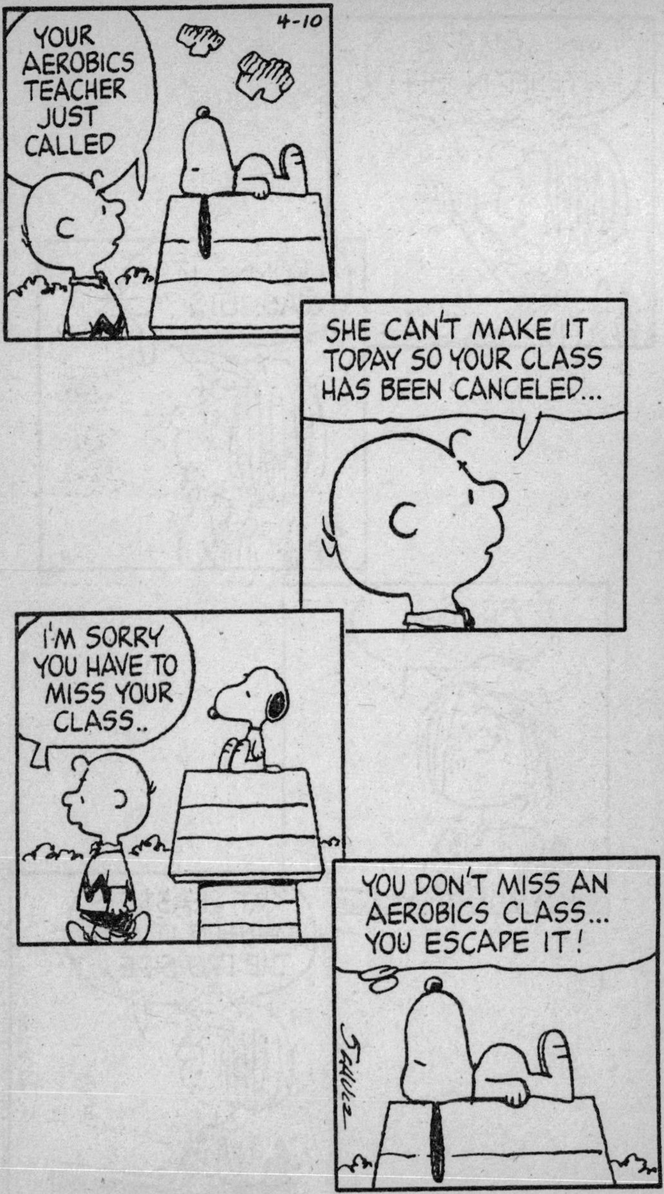
4-10
YOUR AEROBICS TEACHER JUST CALLED
SHE CAN'T MAKE IT TODAY SO YOUR CLASS HAS BEEN CANCELED...
I'M SORRY YOU HAVE TO MISS YOUR CLASS..
YOU DON'T MISS AN AEROBICS CLASS... YOU ESCAPE IT!
SCHULZ

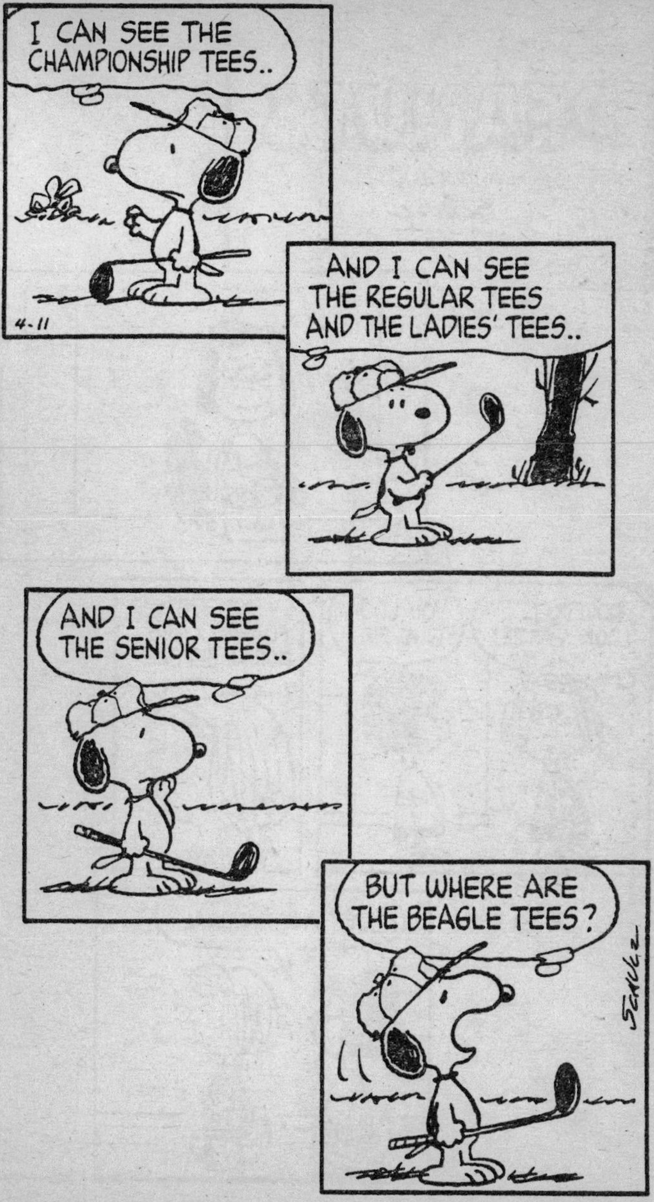
I CAN SEE THE CHAMPIONSHIP TEES..
4-11
AND I CAN SEE THE REGULAR TEES AND THE LADIES' TEES..
AND I CAN SEE THE SENIOR TEES..
BUT WHERE ARE THE BEAGLE TEES?
SCHULZ

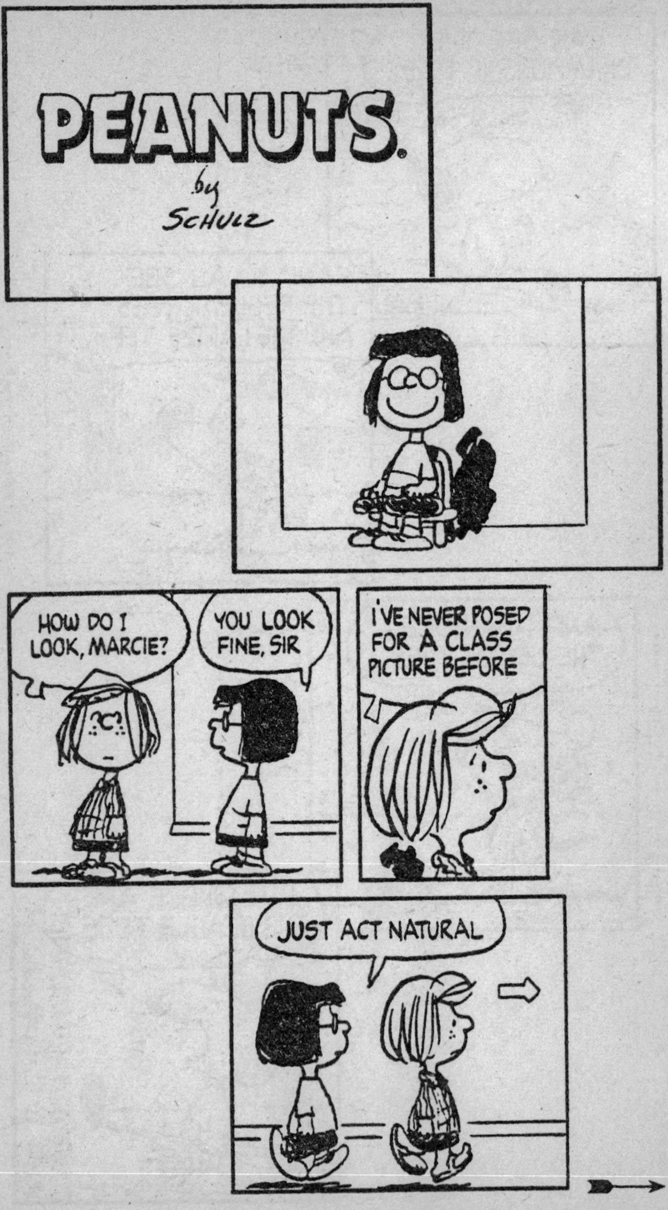
PEANUTS
by SCHULZ
HOW DO I LOOK, MARCIE?
YOU LOOK FINE, SIR
I'VE NEVER POSED FOR A CLASS PICTURE BEFORE
JUST ACT NATURAL

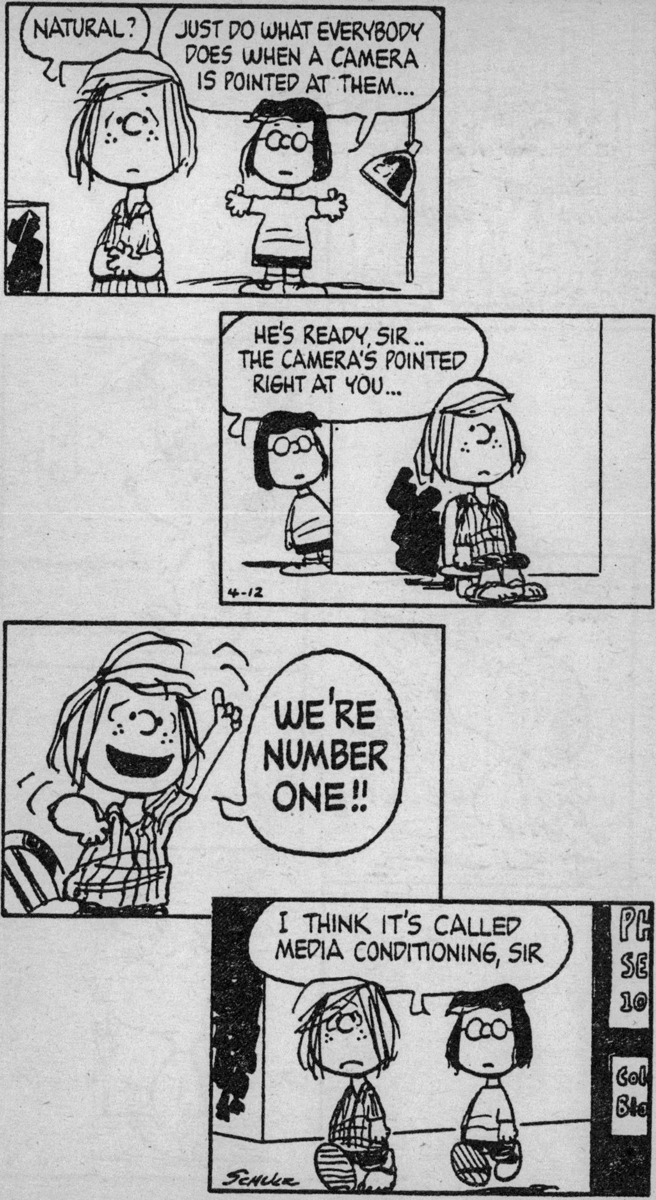
NATURAL?
JUST DO WHAT EVERYBODY DOES WHEN A CAMERA IS POINTED AT THEM...
HE'S READY, SIR.. THE CAMERA'S POINTED RIGHT AT YOU...
4-12
WE'RE NUMBER ONE!!
I THINK IT'S CALLED MEDIA CONDITIONING, SIR
SCHULZ

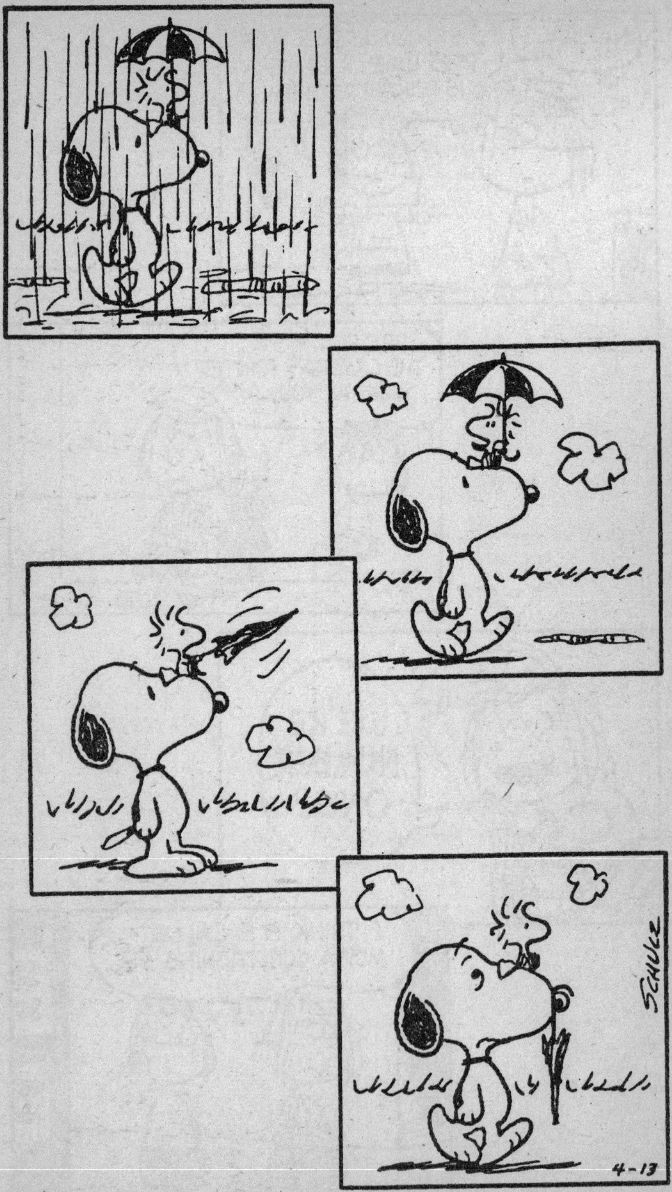
SCHULZ
4-13

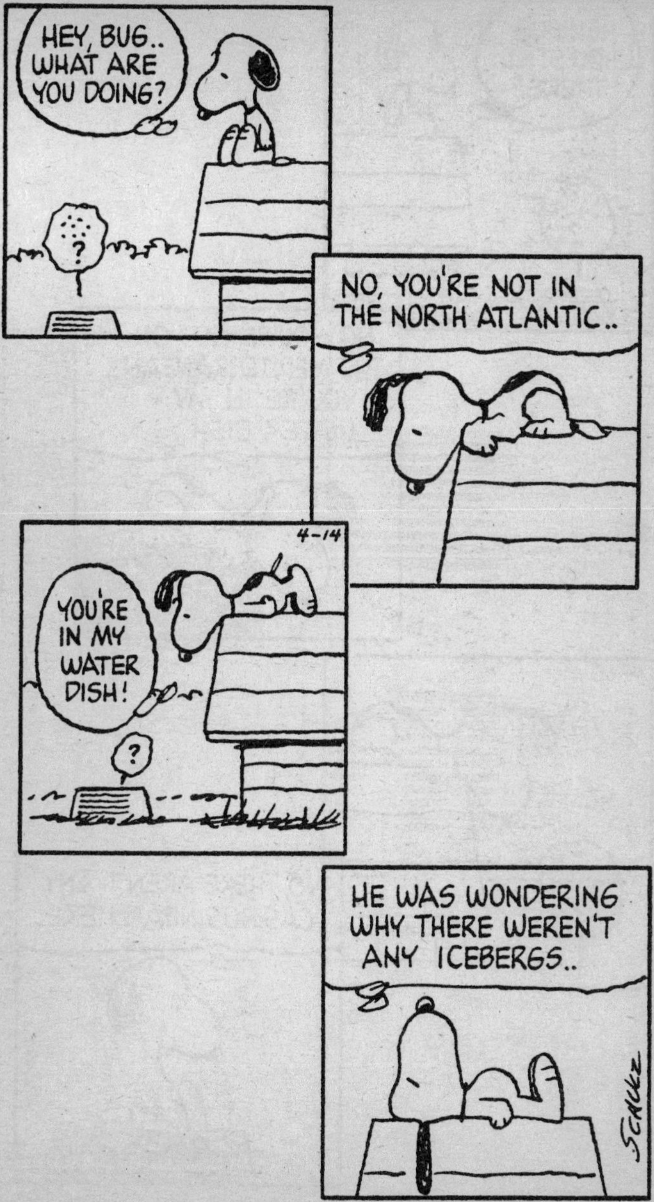
HEY, BUG..
WHAT ARE
YOU DOING?
?
NO, YOU'RE NOT IN
THE NORTH ATLANTIC..
4-14
YOU'RE
IN MY
WATER
DISH!
?
HE WAS WONDERING
WHY THERE WEREN'T
ANY ICEBERGS..
SCHULZ

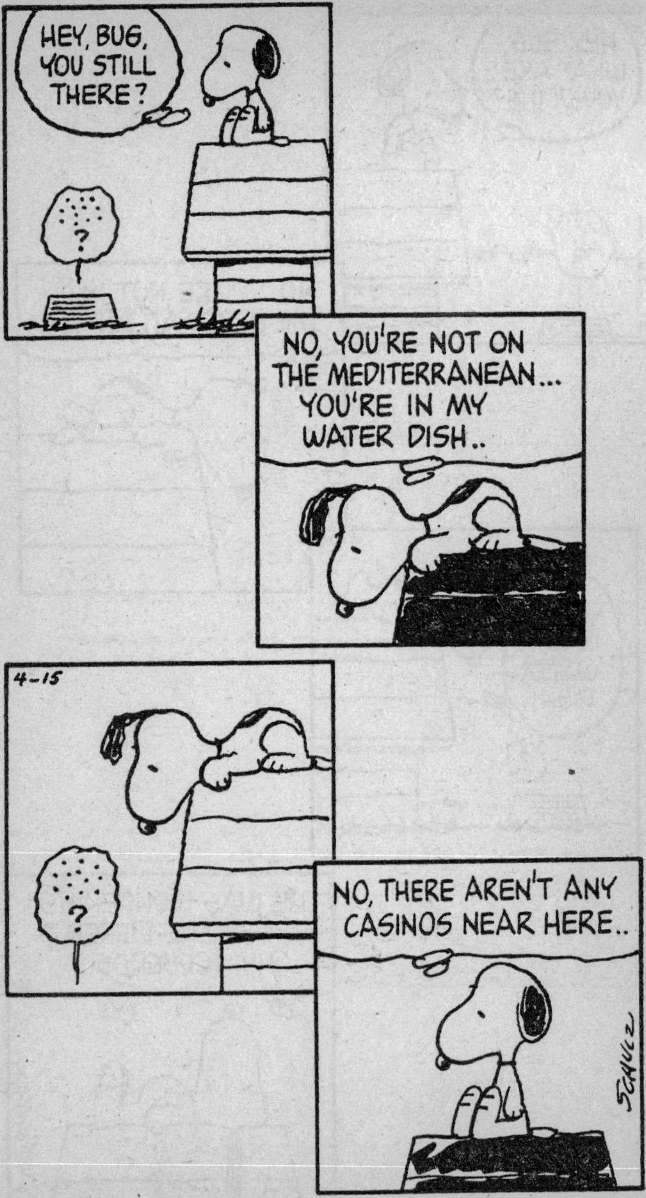
HEY, BUG, YOU STILL THERE?
?
NO, YOU'RE NOT ON THE MEDITERRANEAN... YOU'RE IN MY WATER DISH..
4-15
?
NO, THERE AREN'T ANY CASINOS NEAR HERE..
SCHULZ

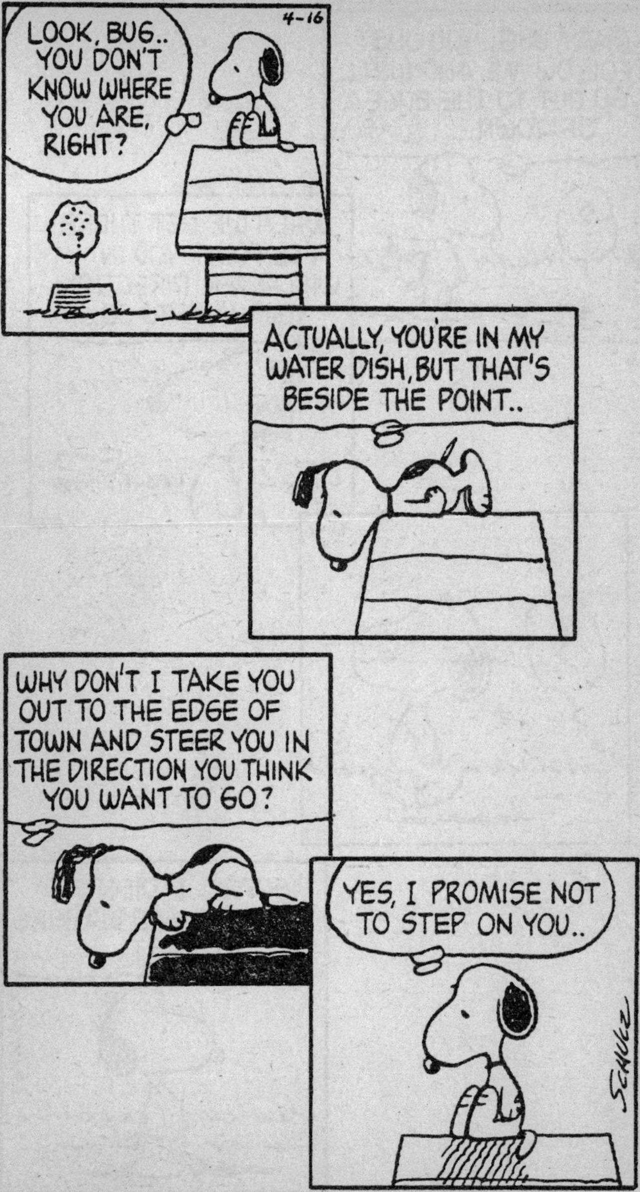
4-16
LOOK, BUG.. YOU DON'T KNOW WHERE YOU ARE, RIGHT?
ACTUALLY, YOU'RE IN MY WATER DISH, BUT THAT'S BESIDE THE POINT..
WHY DON'T I TAKE YOU OUT TO THE EDGE OF TOWN AND STEER YOU IN THE DIRECTION YOU THINK YOU WANT TO GO?
YES, I PROMISE NOT TO STEP ON YOU..
SCHULZ

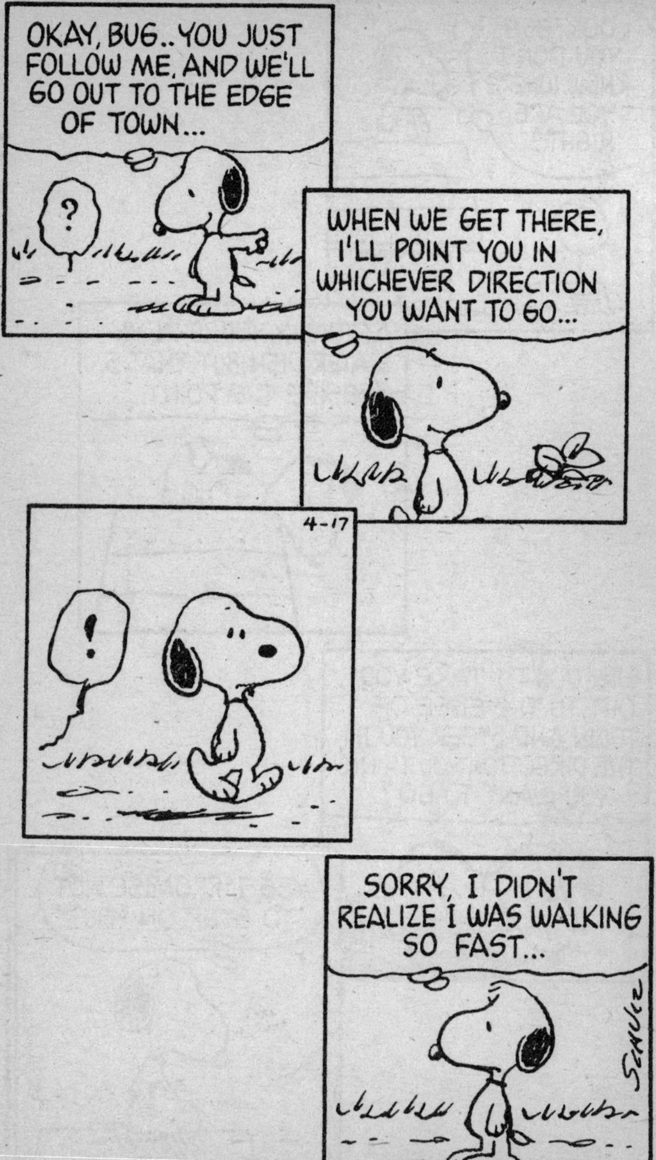
OKAY, BUG.. YOU JUST FOLLOW ME, AND WE'LL GO OUT TO THE EDGE OF TOWN...
?
WHEN WE GET THERE, I'LL POINT YOU IN WHICHEVER DIRECTION YOU WANT TO GO...
4-17
!
SORRY, I DIDN'T REALIZE I WAS WALKING SO FAST...
SCHULZ

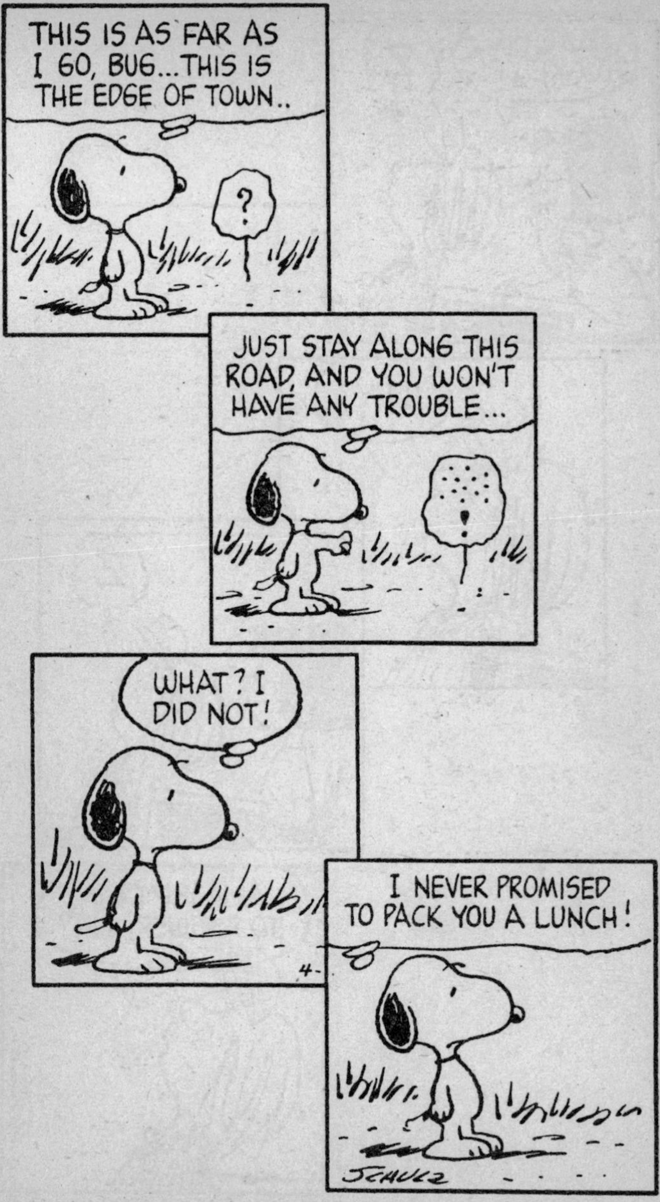
THIS IS AS FAR AS I GO, BUG...THIS IS THE EDGE OF TOWN..
?
JUST STAY ALONG THIS ROAD, AND YOU WON'T HAVE ANY TROUBLE...
WHAT? I DID NOT!
I NEVER PROMISED TO PACK YOU A LUNCH!

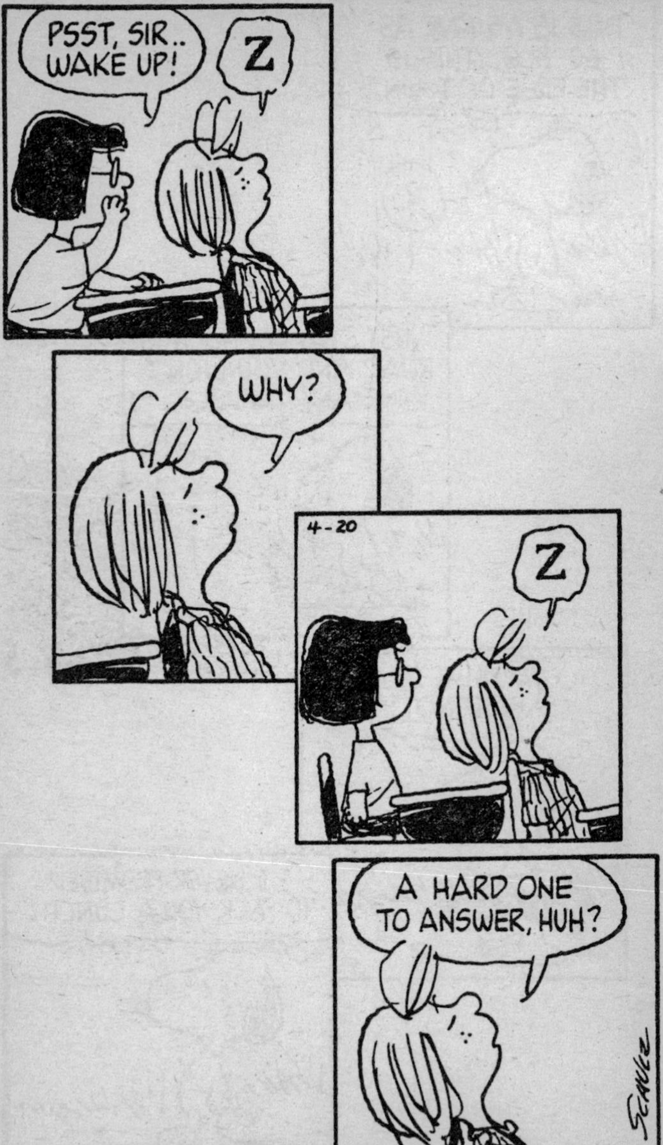
PSST, SIR..
WAKE UP!
Z
WHY?
4-20
Z
A HARD ONE TO ANSWER, HUH?

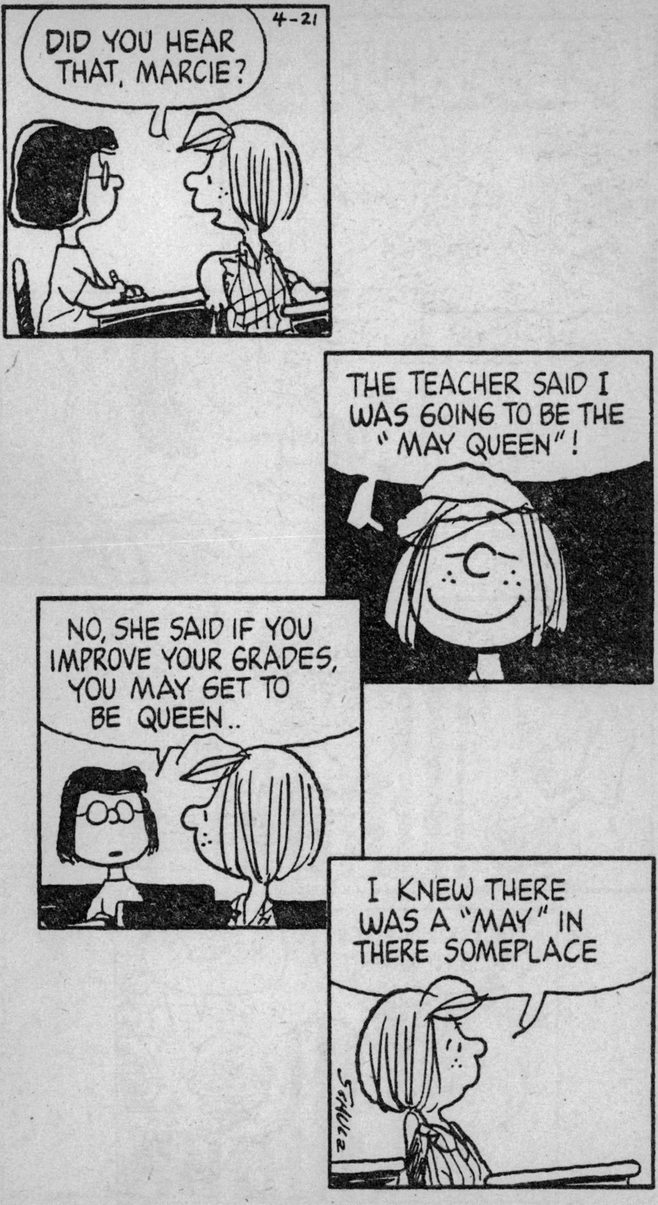
4-21
DID YOU HEAR THAT, MARCIE?
THE TEACHER SAID I WAS GOING TO BE THE "MAY QUEEN"!
NO, SHE SAID IF YOU IMPROVE YOUR GRADES, YOU MAY GET TO BE QUEEN..
I KNEW THERE WAS A "MAY" IN THERE SOMEPLACE
SCHULZ

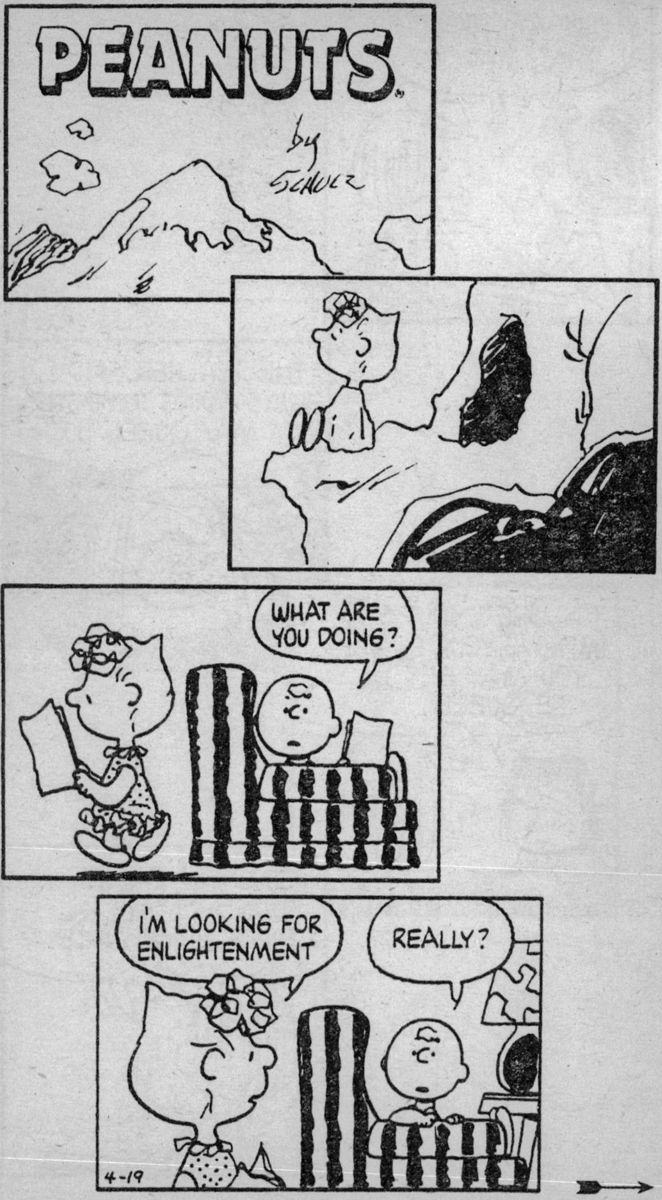
PEANUTS
by SCHULZ
WHAT ARE YOU DOING?
I'M LOOKING FOR ENLIGHTENMENT
REALLY?
4-19

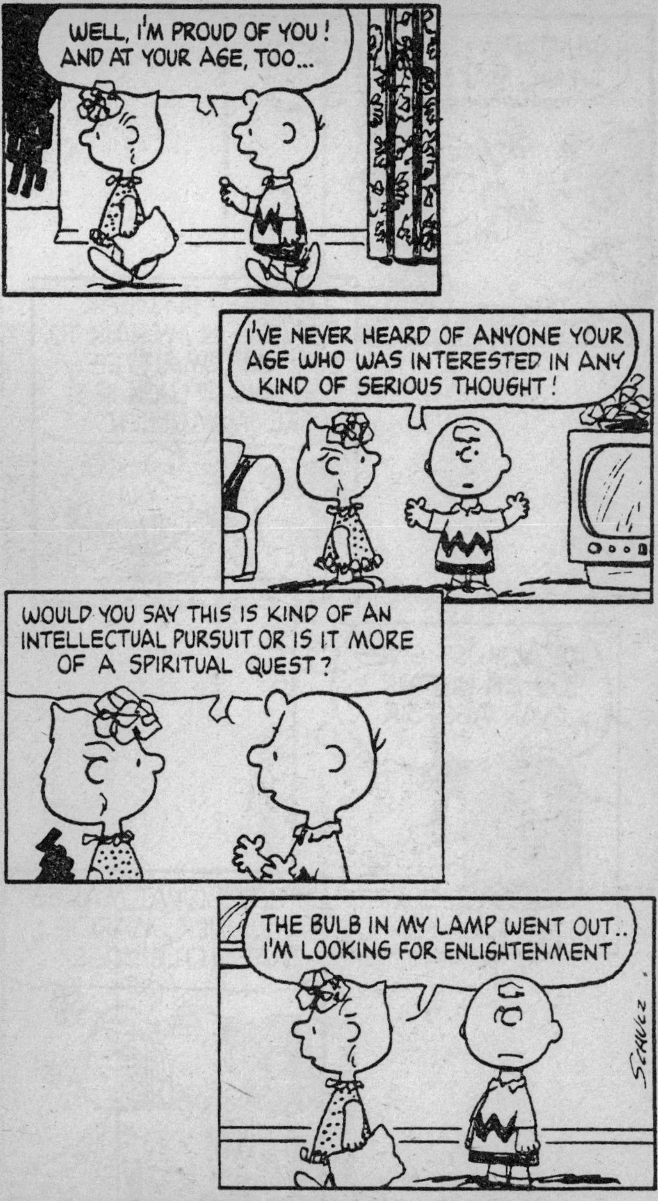
WELL, I'M PROUD OF YOU! AND AT YOUR AGE, TOO...
I'VE NEVER HEARD OF ANYONE YOUR AGE WHO WAS INTERESTED IN ANY KIND OF SERIOUS THOUGHT!
WOULD YOU SAY THIS IS KIND OF AN INTELLECTUAL PURSUIT OR IS IT MORE OF A SPIRITUAL QUEST?
THE BULB IN MY LAMP WENT OUT.. I'M LOOKING FOR ENLIGHTENMENT
SCHULZ

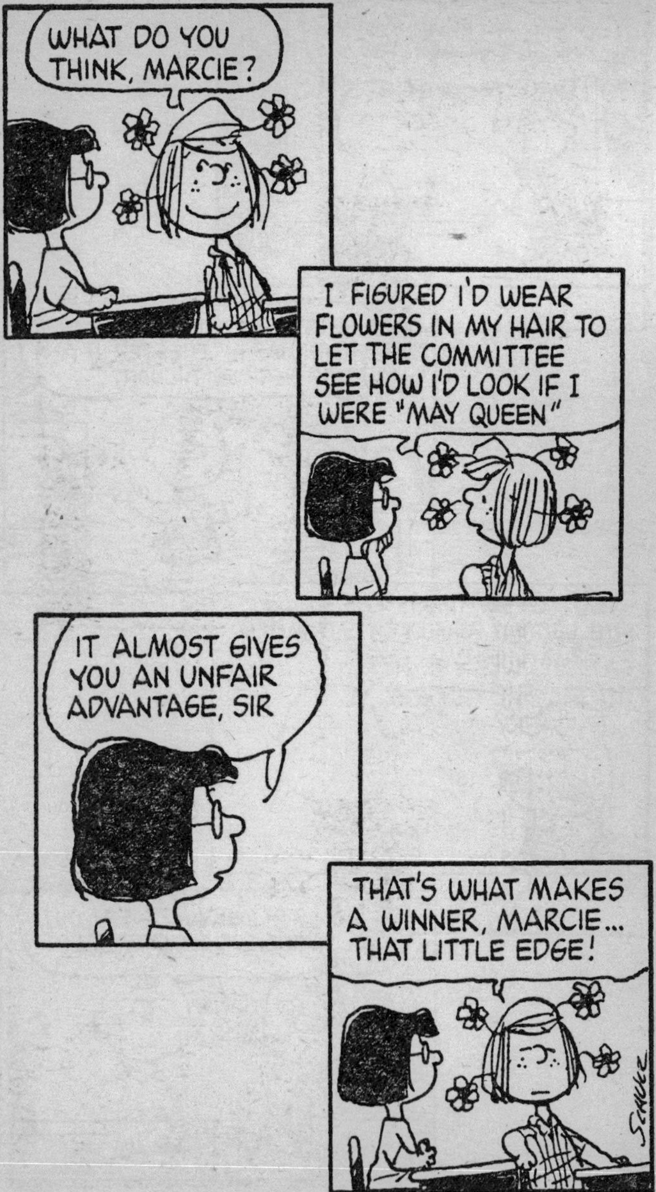
WHAT DO YOU THINK, MARCIE?
I FIGURED I'D WEAR FLOWERS IN MY HAIR TO LET THE COMMITTEE SEE HOW I'D LOOK IF I WERE "MAY QUEEN"
IT ALMOST GIVES YOU AN UNFAIR ADVANTAGE, SIR
THAT'S WHAT MAKES A WINNER, MARCIE... THAT LITTLE EDGE!
SCHULZ

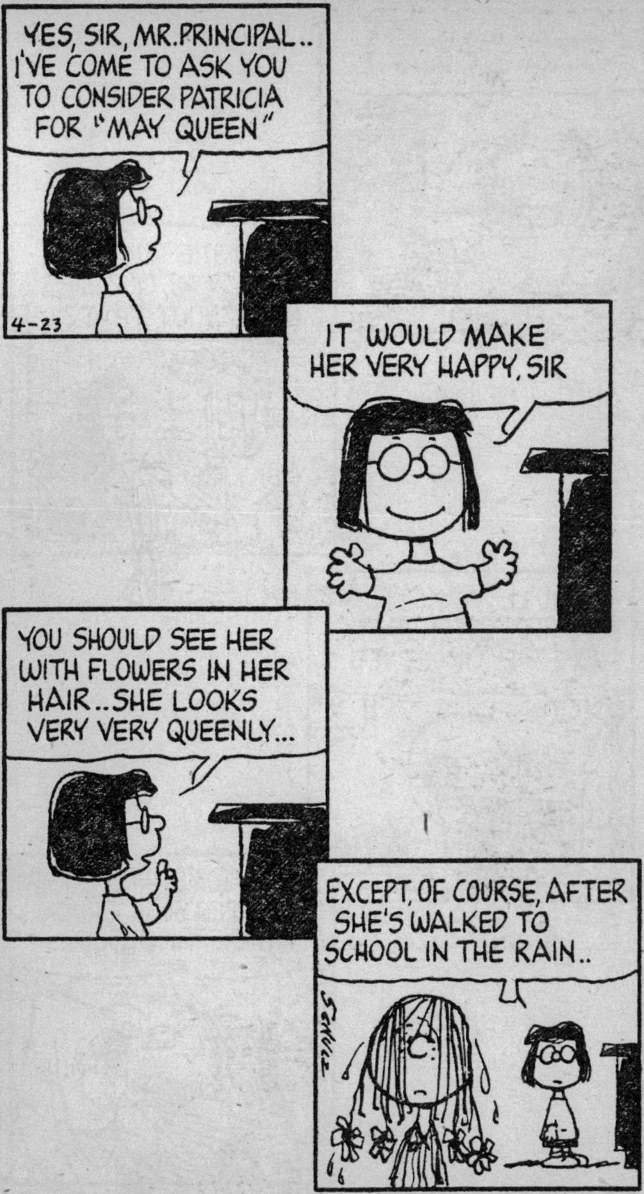
YES, SIR, MR.PRINCIPAL.. I'VE COME TO ASK YOU TO CONSIDER PATRICIA FOR "MAY QUEEN"
4-23
IT WOULD MAKE HER VERY HAPPY, SIR
YOU SHOULD SEE HER WITH FLOWERS IN HER HAIR..SHE LOOKS VERY VERY QUEENLY...
EXCEPT, OF COURSE, AFTER SHE'S WALKED TO SCHOOL IN THE RAIN..
SCHULZ

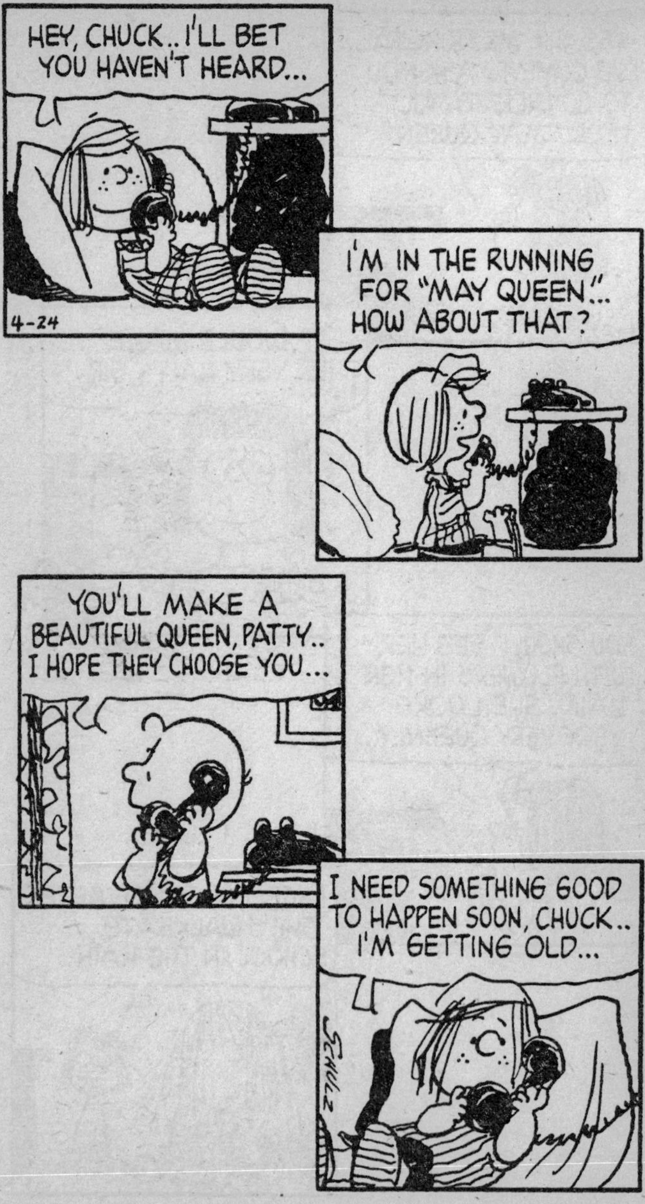
HEY, CHUCK.. I'LL BET YOU HAVEN'T HEARD...
4-24
I'M IN THE RUNNING FOR "MAY QUEEN"... HOW ABOUT THAT?
YOU'LL MAKE A BEAUTIFUL QUEEN, PATTY.. I HOPE THEY CHOOSE YOU...
I NEED SOMETHING GOOD TO HAPPEN SOON, CHUCK.. I'M GETTING OLD...
SCHULZ

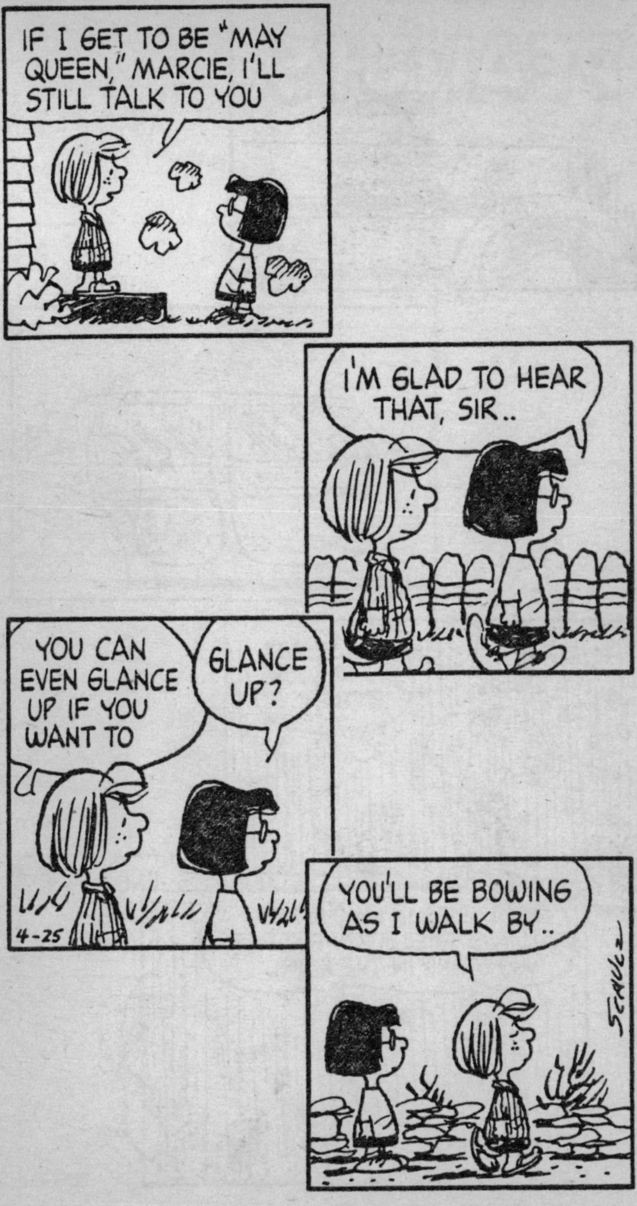
IF I GET TO BE "MAY QUEEN," MARCIE, I'LL STILL TALK TO YOU
I'M GLAD TO HEAR THAT, SIR..
YOU CAN EVEN GLANCE UP IF YOU WANT TO
GLANCE UP?
4-25
YOU'LL BE BOWING AS I WALK BY..
SCHULZ

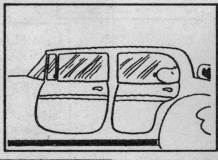

THE SECRET IS TO LOOK PATHETIC..

RICH LADIES IN LIMOUSINES ALWAYS FEEL SORRY FOR DOGS WHO STAND IN THE RAIN..

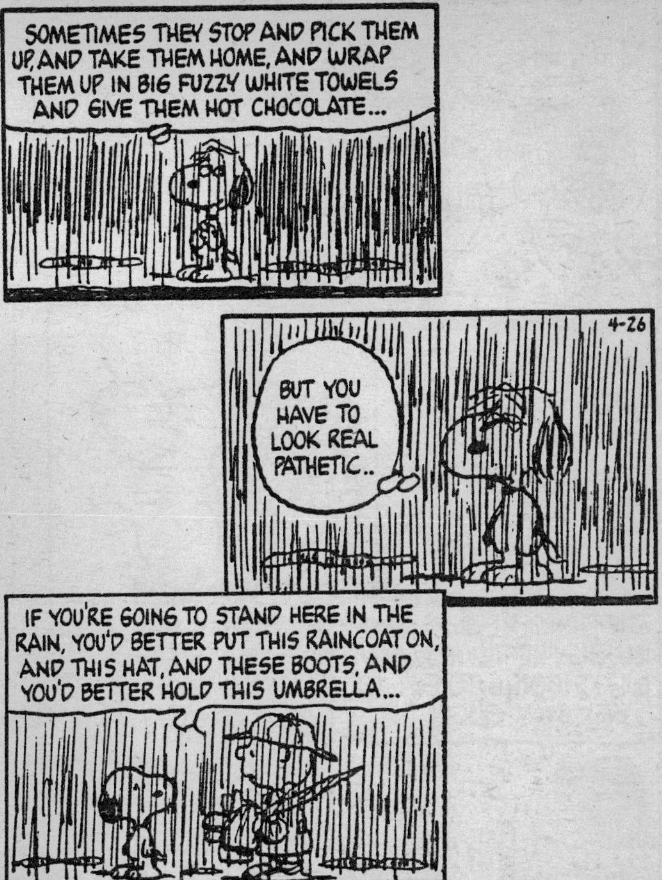

SOMETIMES THEY STOP AND PICK THEM UP, AND TAKE THEM HOME, AND WRAP THEM UP IN BIG FUZZY WHITE TOWELS AND GIVE THEM HOT CHOCOLATE...
4-26
BUT YOU HAVE TO LOOK REAL PATHETIC..
IF YOU'RE GOING TO STAND HERE IN THE RAIN, YOU'D BETTER PUT THIS RAINCOAT ON, AND THIS HAT, AND THESE BOOTS, AND YOU'D BETTER HOLD THIS UMBRELLA...
SO MUCH FOR PATHETIC!

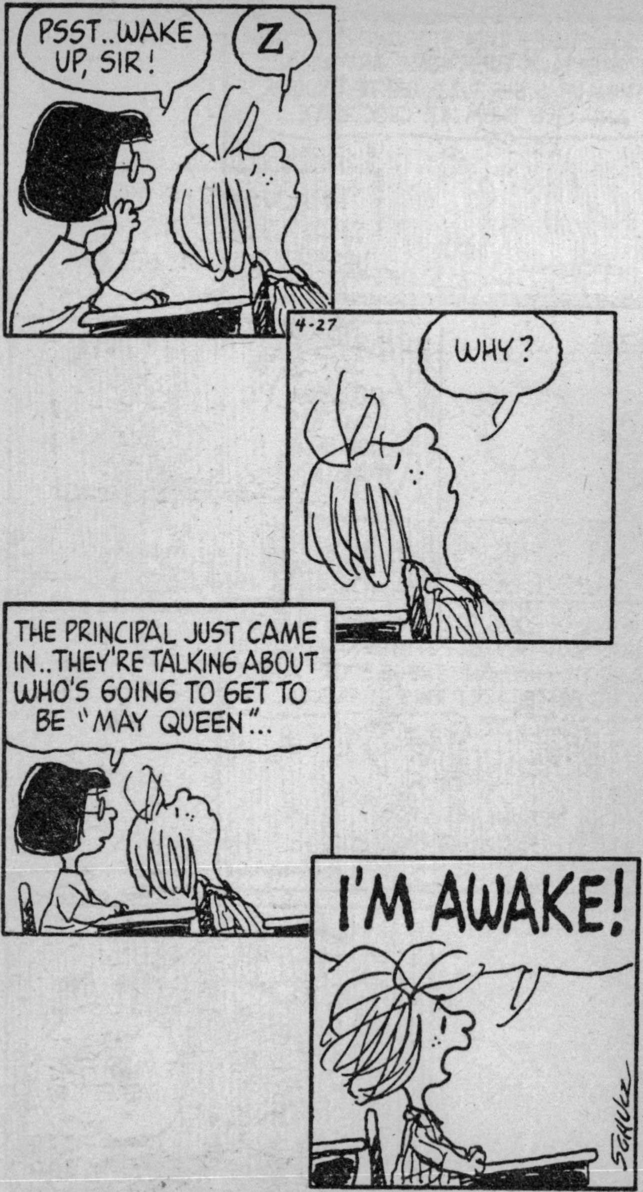
PSST..WAKE UP, SIR!
Z
4-27
WHY?
THE PRINCIPAL JUST CAME IN..THEY'RE TALKING ABOUT WHO'S GOING TO GET TO BE "MAY QUEEN"...
I'M AWAKE!
SCHULZ

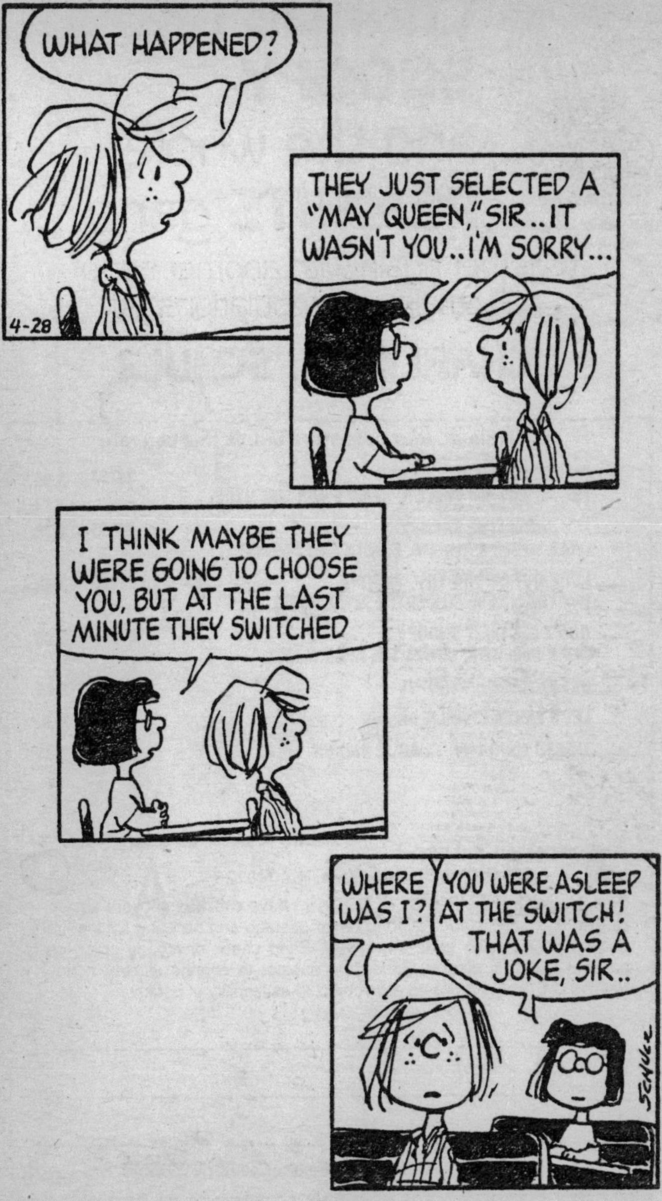
WHAT HAPPENED?
4-28
THEY JUST SELECTED A "MAY QUEEN," SIR..IT WASN'T YOU..I'M SORRY...
I THINK MAYBE THEY WERE GOING TO CHOOSE YOU, BUT AT THE LAST MINUTE THEY SWITCHED
WHERE WAS I?
YOU WERE ASLEEP AT THE SWITCH! THAT WAS A JOKE, SIR..
SCHULZ

Copr. © 1952
United Feature Syndicate, Inc.

CHARLIE BROWN, SNOOPY
and the whole
PEANUTS® gang...

together again with another set of
daily trials and tribulations by

CHARLES M. SCHULZ